This copy of *You. Change. Now!*

is presented to:

I believe in your gifts and talents and stand in agreement for

your *complete success* - Mentally, Spiritually, Socially, Physically,

and Financially.

By:

Brandon Clay Enterprises, LLC

You. Change. Now!

7-Day Life Transformation Program

Define Your Goals, Conquer Your Fears, Take Control of Your Life and Achieve Your Personal Best!

Brandon L. Clay
www.brandonlclay.com

This publication is designed to provide accurate and authoritative information in regard to the subject matter covered. It is sold with the understanding that the publisher and author are not engaged in rendering legal, accounting, or other professional services. If legal advice or other expert assistance is required, the services of a competent professional should be sought.

Published by Brandon Clay Enterprises, LLC
McDonough, GA
www.brandonlclay.com

You. Change Now! – *7-Day Life Transformation Program is* the 3rd^d updated version of Brandon Clay's original **10 Power Principals of Success** (1996) & the **You. Change. Now! Program** (2010)

For ordering information or special discounts for bulk purchases, please email Brandon Clay Enterprises, LLC at orders@brandonlclay.com

Design and composition by Brandon Clay Enterprises, LLC
Cover Design by Brandon Clay Enterprises, LLC

This work and *everything* I do is dedicated to my best friend and wife, Natalie. All my love and devotion!

To the millions of people, worldwide, who are pursuing greatness that may happen upon one of my works: I believe in the nobility of sales and your ability to be a top professional. My greatest desire is that something said within these pages will impact your life and set you on course to unleash all the greatness that is within you!

I wish you Money, Power, and Success!

Additional Titles Available from Brandon L Clay;

Sales Crumbs Trilogy – *the definitive guide to sales success and life mastery!*
Volume I - Sales Crumbs from the Master's Table
Volume II - A Trail of Sales Crumbs
Volume III - Feasting On Sales Crumbs

Your Authentic Sales Voice - *Discovering and unleashing your most natural gift for greater sales success!*

S=ME²- *Revolutionary Success Formula!*

The 80% Sales Solution - *Training program based on the popular Sales Crumbs Trilogy*

All titles available in e-book and paperback on Amazon.com and other online retailers!

Table of Contents

<u>Welcome to You.</u> *Change.* Now!

Congratulations on your decision to improve the quality of your life. Think of that word - Decision. According to Webster, *to decide* means to "to make a final choice or judgment". Another way to look at it - **decision is the opposite of incision**. Incision means to "cut into", decision means to "cut off from". If I have the proper insight into why you are the possessor of this program, it is probably because you are ready to "cut off from" something you no longer want to tolerate in your life. Whatever it is, this transformational system can help you break free and achieve a higher level of success!

The program you hold in your hands represents over 30 years of my personal study of people and success. I have witnessed this program change people from all walks of life, and I am confident it will do the same for you. I am humbled and honored to be given the opportunity, and I personally guarantee that the information included can help unleash **the power to change!**

To come clean...I am not so naive or arrogant to believe that I created the "success formula" that is the foundation of this system. It is preceded by a bounty of writings and observations from the past. From an early age I had a desire to succeed, and during high school became a student of the success classics. I was influenced by the powerful writings and concepts dispensed by the *vintage masters*...Napoleon Hill, James Allen, Catherine Ponder, Joseph Murphy, Charles Haanel, Robert Collier, H. Emilie Cady and Wallace Wattles. I was also reliant on the teachings of the Bible and its instruction on living life abundantly. The experiences of the past 30 years have helped me assemble this system as a contemporary culmination of all those basic, time-tested truths.

In this updated version of my original **<u>10 Power Principles of Success Program</u>** (1995), I have endeavored to do one thing...**help you live your best life possible!** The original program was 30 days and took the participant through a "deep dive" of success philosophies and technologies. The last 15 years of leading 100's of people through the original program have taught me that not everyone needs, *or wants*, ALL the details.

I recently purchased a new Corvette – the 2014 Stingray. I still own the 2009 Corvette as well – both are stunning to look at and exhilarating to drive (within the speed limits, of course!). I read the owner's manual to make sure I understood how *special* things worked...the air conditioner, radio, Cd player, etc. I was not as interested in the engine, brakes, and transmission...someone <u>much</u> smarter than me engineered the car in such a way that a non-gearhead like me could drive the car and enjoy its power, *immediately*. In this new version of my program, I am simply "handing you the keys to the car".

I have condensed the 30 day program into 7 power-packed sessions to give you all the essentials you need for success. As in my Corvette analogy, there are some things I know as a driver of *any* car - keys, gas, brakes. There are things I have to learn - sound system, climate control, and special settings. But the really intensely technical items, like horsepower, ventilated braking systems, and carbon fiber monocoque frame are engineering marvels that I must "trust" will adhere to the established laws of physics. This program takes the same approach. I know that you understand *your life*, and that you now need to learn the "special" things that can increase your enjoyment of that life. While the program provides an overview of the technical laws of success, it won't bury you in them, but rather give you enough to understand them and more importantly, **<u>trust them</u>**.

I also realize that 7 days isn't enough time to lose those 10 pounds (safely anyway!), amass your first million dollars (lottery notwithstanding!), or go back to college for your Master's Degree. My goal for these 7 days is to spark change in the first place it must occur...*in your mind and thinking!* The chapters are designed to build on the mental syntax of change and give you permission to design your life as you would like to live it - to empower you. Then there are workshops that are designed to make you think about your life in ways you may never have before. As you begin to see your life differently (insight) you will propel to a better future destiny (foresight).

It is time to get started and to reach any destination, one must begin the journey with only one intention - *to arrive!* Look deep within yourself and find the courage and strength to commit to **You. *Change.* Now!** for the next 7 days. The results will amaze you! I know that you are anxious to get started. I stand in agreement with you that all you desire and deserve will be manifested as a result of this program. I wish you Money, Power, and Success!

Day One – Elevate Your Mind!

The mind, once expanded to the dimensions of larger
ideas, never returns to its original size.
Oliver Wendell Holmes

Welcome to Day One! I hope you are as excited as I am about the valuable time we will get to spend together for the next 7 days (*and hopefully beyond*)! If you are like most people, you have some anxiety about getting started with this type of program. *Will it work? Will I really change?* By my definition, anxiety is simply 99% excitement and 1% fear of the unknown. **Don't worry, that anxiety only makes you human!**

This system is designed to take all the wondrous characteristics of your human nature and through the use of specific tools and exercises help **you change!** Without ever meeting you there are some things I know without a doubt…

What I know about You!

I know that **You** are an incredibly unique creation that has abilities and gifts that once you recognize them and present them to the world, will provide a two way street of great value! Once you get hold of the fact that there is a unique audience for your talents, you will be compelled to hone those talents and ready them for the inevitable "Great Performance". If you are like most people, you are doubtful or even afraid to use the best parts of who you are in service to the world. This fear is fundamental to the *Human Experience*. Our greatest gifts are latent and hidden behind a wall of self-doubt and insecurity. **It is time to shake off the fear and give yourself credit for who you were really meant to be!** I know that greatness resides on the inside of you, and I know this program can help to uncover and unleash that greatness!

What I know about Change!

I know that *Change* is a source of great fear for most people. Ironically, in order to achieve and receive the things you want in life, change is the primary vehicle! Changing professions, relationships, or other "stable" areas of your life is difficult because fear of the unknown will paralyze you...keep you in your current place... perpetuate complacency and mediocrity. Change as the vehicle of achievement is positive, it is nurturing, and necessary. Most critical for you to understand is that change is inevitable. **Thankfully, change is under your control, even if it is only you controlling the *reaction* you have to change!** When you look back on times where you felt "out of control" of change, that change was likely necessary to take you to another level. *Ultimately, change is what takes you to your destiny!* Welcome it and be the catalyst for it!

What I know about Now!

I know that **Now** is immediate, it is urgent, it *obliterates procrastination.* A casual wish or lukewarm desire creates a need, but not a need that must be fulfilled, *immediately.* The desire to find a job if you are unhappy in your current position may not generate the intense, white heat of desire that motivates you to action. **But *lose* that job and the desire becomes so pressing, so imperative, that now is a mandate!** When the need is great enough, or the desire is of a significant magnitude, now rushes in to meet the need, or fulfill the desire. Tomorrow is good for *some* things, but if its appearance is required and mandatory, now is all that matters!

What I know about You. *Change.* Now!!

Because of my own life and the lives of countless others who have benefited from the concepts in this program, I am confident in your ability to use this system as the driver of helping you become who you were destined to become. Once you grasp who **You.** are, that *Change.* is your ally, and that **Now** is ever present, you are well on your way to evolving beautifully and masterfully toward your ultimate destiny. As humans, who were designed for accomplishment, there are five fundamental areas that encompass the whole of our existence… the fulfillment of our basic human needs can be measured in these areas (In no particular order):

Financial ~ Spiritual ~ Mental ~ Physical ~ Social

Fab Five

I like to refer to these as the Fab Five. To live a life of true happiness and meaning, we need to evolve in every area. No one area should be deemed more important that the other. Yes, I know that some people place great value on financial, but challenge them with health issues and the pendulum swings to physical. To enjoy a full and "charmed" life, you need balance in all areas of the Fab Five. Let's take a closer look at these areas:

1. **Financial** - With the current economic challenges that so many face, I understand this area is getting more attention and focus - mainly in a negative way. *Our economic well being is directly tied to how we feel in all the other areas of our lives.* Rather than complain about the rules of the game changing, we need to "step up our game" and get our finances handled and in order. Thankfully, financial laws are strictly "mathematical" and will work for anyone that applies them. You will have to stop being afraid, lazy, and complacent to make this happen...the world is now a global marketplace and 6 billion people are now woven together economically. Given the challenges, I know that some people are putting dreams "on hold" and waiting for "better times". *I say "Forget That!"* *Opportunities are not diminishing for people of*

innovation and ambition. Those 6 billion people still have desires that need to be met, and problems that need to be solved...**they are waiting on your gifts!** This is the time to dream and *dream big* so that the visions in your mind get BIGGER than the challenges that exisit. On the higher side of the challenges is still a land of Milk and Honey!

2. **Spiritual** - In an expanding world, the concept of spirituality is now becoming one of taboo, or great debate. The beauty of true spiritualism is that it is *intensely* personal, and untouchable by outside forces. In its simplest form, it is our moral and values "center" that anchors us in times of tribulation and jubilation. At the more complex end is religion, doctrine, and belief systems ranging from atheistic - agnostic - devout - heretic. *Even within the same organized religion, two people will interpret scriptures in different ways.* That is because you were uniquely designed to "hear" in a specific way. While I have my own specific belief system, this program won't condemn others or "preach" *(though I did that for 5 years!)* because the only important thing for you to recognize is *who* you are and Truth will be revealed in the journey... when your hunger for the answer is intense enough. **There is great peace and fulfillment to be found internally that can propel you to greatness.**

3. **Mental -** Would you consider yourself an optimist, pessimist or something in between? Your view of the world and the possiblities it holds for you is deeply rooted in your mental perception of it. Your will is a vital part of who you are and is a powerful determiner of if/what you will accomplish in life. Your capacity to observe conditions, learn the things that are important

to your success, make qualified choices and to focus on critical tasks are all elements of your mental life. Mental development is not simply about I.Q or whether you made all "A's" in school...in fact, scholastic acumen (skill) is a poor measure of if someone will be successful or not. It is the person that can filter out the distractions, remain laser focused on their gifts and conversion of those gifts in service to mankind that will achieve at the highest levels. Business philosopher Jim Rohn puts it simply, *"Formal education will make you a living, self-education will make you a fortune"*.

4. **Physical** - *Darn those last 10lbs, I want the Dairy Queen double Heath Blizzard!* Yes, most of us fight the battle of the bulge, as evidenced by the billions of dollars spent in the pursuit of a youthful, svelte physique! While vanity is not "vain" (we all want to be a "10"...*at least to one person...right?*), the true benefit of adopting a better lifestyle is good health. The obesity epidemic is serious and is robbing people of energy, finances, and the overall health required to live a full and abundant life. The desire to fit into the jeans of your twenties is admirable *and* achievable, but consider yourself fortunate if that is your greatest physical challenge. Understand that physical achievement is a mindset that translates into a *lifestyle* and opens the door to vibrancy and unbounding energy and that is a pre-requisite for ultimate success.

5. **Social** - No man is an island and we **all** need people. Wouldn't it be great if everyone thought the way *we did*, liked the things *we liked*, and we all just "got along"? Of course, it is not that simple! We have family, friends, colleagues, and strangers that we have to interact with on a daily basis and that "social network" is now

more accessible than ever. Facebook, Twitter, and other social media have given the entire world a view into our private and personal lives. These various forms of social interaction can be used to announce the birth of a child, or the birth of a business, and millions can react...instantly! Face to face or through technology, the impact you have on your immediate and expanded world will play an important role in your success and the enjoyment along the way.

While we will always focus and place great emphasis on creating balance in all of the Fab Five, there is another more concise view of what makes for an abundant life. Quite simply they are:

Money ~ Power ~ Success

For every human desire and aspiration, witin the Fab Five, one of these three words can sum up what we are attempting to manifest. Dispel any immediate reaction that says "I am above such egocentric and ignoble desires". It is old, misguided definitions that have placed negative connotations to these primary requirements of life. Which of these can you live without? While not everyone wants to be rich, we all require money on some level... even if we are relying on strangers to eat ... *they* had to have money to give! So rather than fight over semantics, let's define these three words in such a way as to reassure us that the pursuit of them is indeed noble and good!

♫ Money, Money, Money, Money.... (*Money!*)

Money is one of the most emotional words known to man. People will steal, kill, and destroy to attain it. For most, it is an object to be wished for, not acquired in large amounts. We are told that the "rich get richer" from the labor of the little man. Let the truth be told about money - *it is simply a convenient way to demonstrate an exchange of value between people.* **The way to make more money is to find a way to create and increase value.**

I Got The Power!

Like money, power is a misunderstood term. Webster defines power as "the ability to act effectively". The ability to do anything comes from knowledge. Knowledge is acquired by experience, attention, and study. Many people have various types of knowledge, but not *acting* on that knowledge, does not translate it into power. **If we want more power, we must begin to obtain and act, effectively, on knowledge.**

A Great Success!

Success has traditionally been measured by the amount of money someone has amassed. The size of their home, the type of car they drive, or the clothes they wear. In truth, success should mean different things to each individual. It is simply the ability to live life on your own terms and agenda. The accumulation of wealth is not the most important factor in defining if you have achieved success. **Waking up to a tomorrow that is filled with your dreams in all of the Fab Five areas is the true measure of success.**

A Wasted Mind is a Terrible Thing!

Money, Power, and Success - three of the most commanding forces known to man. These 7 days are about every area of your life...*your* Money, *your* Power and *your* Success. Our mission is to impart proven strategies and techniques to create a new reality for your life.

As with all knowledge (the pre-requisite of power), we must begin with your brain – more specifically, *your mind.* The mind is our super computer for processing all the information the universe has to offer – and it is offering it at lightning speed for the person willing to tap into its vast resources of knowledge, opportunity, and wisdom.

Most people are unaware that they have pre-programmed, physiological responses to money, power and success. Their thoughts (mentally held images or beliefs) are based on life experiences or what they have been taught. For most people, these automatic responses, whether they be positive or negative, are the result of conditioning. Conditioning is a result of **repeated actions** that "anchor" themselves in your mind until your reaction to them is no longer in your conscious control – *they become automatic and involuntary*. Your thoughts become robotic and predictable and will dictate your action, or worse, your inaction as it relates to money, power, and success.

Alpo Time!

Ivan Pavlov was a Russian Physiologist that conducted experiments (no animals were harmed!) on dogs. Essentially, at time of feedings, he would "ring the bell"…then feed the dogs. He continued, "ring the bell"…feed the dogs. Without deviation to the pattern he would, "ring the bell"…feed the dogs. "Ring the bell"…feed the dogs, "ring the bell"…feed the dogs. "Ring the bell"…(did you think "feed the dogs"?). If so, then you were just a "victim" of Pavlovian conditioning or what he deemed "Conditional Reflex".

Conditional Reflex - Cause and Effect

Conditional Reflex is the process by which responses (effect) to a particular stimulus (cause) is automatic and habitual. In the instances where Pavlov "rang the bell" (stimulus – cause) but DID NOT feed the dogs, their physiological responses were driven by conditioning that "bell ringing" *automatically meant eating*. In the absence of physical food, the dogs exhibited all the same behavior as if food <u>was present</u>. In future years, Pavlov built this Conditional Reflex correlation to human behavior - that is you and me!

To test this theory, think of something that is very tart to the taste…like a lemon, a kosher pickle, or one of the insanely sour candies that kids love so much. If you think intensely enough, the memory (cause - stimulus) *alone* can create a set of physiological responses (effect – Conditional Reflex). Your lips pucker, your glands begin to secret saliva to fight off the potency of the sour flavor – just as if you had it in your mouth. Think you can fight it? Have a friend take a handful of salt and slowly lick it in your presence! "Ring the bell"…(yeah, you thought it!)

Gateway to the Mind – The Five Physical Senses

Think of your Conditional Reflex to the sour food. It is based on your experience and data gathered over a lifetime. This data was supplied to your mind through the gateways of the five physical senses of **touch, taste, smell, sight and sound**. The conscious mind provides the access to *"reality data"* and the sub-conscious mind can create *"fantasy world data"* to re-create the sensations even if the stimulus is **not real**…*only imagined!* More about that process later. For now, understand that your mind has established thoughts about money, power, and success that are in large part automatic Conditional Reflexes. Think of various amounts of money (stimulus – cause) and your immediate internal thoughts (effects – Conditional Reflex):

What if someone asked you to borrow the amount?
What if someone gave you the amount?

When it comes to someone asking you for money, if you are honest with yourself, as the amounts get higher, your thoughts drift toward negativity and your <u>inability to part with it</u>…or even having the amount to begin with!!! Someone asking for $5 to buy lunch is not likely to generate the same response as someone asking for $500 for their car payment. At a certain point, your response to their request is even dismissed totally as you know you have no ability to give it (or earn it) in the first place. A friend asking for $5,000 when you have it is troubling, them asking for $5 million is comical!

Strangely, you are likely to have the same progressive reactions to someone giving you money. The lower amounts are "easy" and the higher amounts become more difficult to reconcile, mentally. Your aunt Gertrude giving you $100 for your birthday is exciting, but hearing that she is leaving you $1 million dollars will take a few minutes to adjust to...but I think you would quickly make that adjustment!

As it relates to your ability to become a money magnet, *negative thoughts will repel money and positive thoughts will attract it.* While counterintuitive on many levels, talent is not the best measure of the ability to obtain money, power or success. It is those people who condition themselves to believe themselves worthy and who will take action, that make the most progress. That is why money, power, and success is relative. To the billionaire, to be down to their last $100 million would seem like abject poverty. To the hourly laborer, having $100,000 in savings would feel like King Solomon. We all have the numbers in our head that bring comfort and conversely, discomfort...it is that place of mental "inflection" where real change and progress is made...*let's examine it!*

Mental Sticking Point (M.S.P)

Your Mental Sticking Point (MSP) is based upon your perception (conditioning) of what amount of money, happiness, or achievement is beyond your reach. It is largely determined by your inner programming, the thoughts you hold deeply about your ability to obtain good things in all of the Fab Five areas. **These deeply held beliefs are essentially your self-image.** Even for people that have strong positive self-images, their M.S.P is typically operating at 50%, or less, of their *actual ability*. For example, if someone by conditioning and self-image see themselves maxing out at $250,000 a year, they likely have gifts and abilities that could immediately earn them **double** that amount or $500,000.

M.S.P inherently places more value on words like million and billion and moves them "out of reach". For example, most people are drawn to " ¼ million dollars" as opposed to "five hundred thousand dollars"...even though five hundred thousand is a *higher* number. Most people have established self-induced limitations, based on a mental assessment of their history, ideals they have been exposed to, or their environment. The good news...your M.S.P. in any area of your life can be changed! Yes, despite what your current mental limitations (M.S.P) may dictate, you **can** obtain the perfect weight, have "10" level relationships, and become a multi-millionaire. **You. *Change.* Now!** will help you make those assessments and "move the needle"...guaranteed!

A Common Case of Comma-itis

If we reduce the root cause of your M.S.P. to one common theme, it is *Comma-itis.* Ok, a cute play on words but one that afflicts **everyone** (yes, including me!) in some form or another. *What is Comma-itis?* In some cases, it is a financial condition that limits the ability to think in terms of large numbers. In other cases, it is a physical condition that tells us losing those first 10 pounds, or the last 10, *is impossible.*

While some areas of our lives are more qualitative than quantitative, our subliminal (mental) measurement of certain areas of our lives are subject to M.S.P. For example, happiness is qualitative and subjective, but some days you might feel like a 3 on a scale of 1-10 and other days you feel like an 11! Some people can't see their lives <u>ever</u> being past a 7 on the "happiness" meter...because that is their M.S.P. To understand how Comma-itis effects your wealth *potential,* let's look at how a number is constructed? Look at the number below:

1000000

While the "1" sets the stage, the zeros *potentially* set the magnitude - what is required to make a proper financial number, is to use commas. Let's look at that same number another way:

10,000.00

Same number but with comma (and period) we have created ten thousand. Let's try again:

$$1,000,000$$

Of course, this number is one million (even without the period and the standard two zeros).

How do you react to these numbers... *where* **would you put the comma?** Some people have trouble thinking on the plane of 10,000 and others can *only* think on the plane of million and others...*a billion* . It gets even more complicated when you add a dollar sign! A million grains of sand is not difficult to imagine, but a million dollars begins to have another physiological effect....ring the bell...you get the idea! Think of your reaction to the following numbers that all have the same number of zeros, but with a different value (driven by where the comma is placed):

$$10.00 \text{ vs } \$1,000$$
$$10,000.00 \text{ vs } \$1,000,000$$
$$1.000000000 \text{ vs } \$1,000,000,000$$

Elevating Your Mind is about learning where you put the comma today, and moving it tomorrow! ***Where was your comma-itis diagnosed...*** 1,000, 10,000? Be prepared to move that comma...***today!***

Power of Expectations

Simply put, you get out of life *exactly* what you expect. **The key to growth and development is to change our level of expectations in every area of our lives (Fab Five).** In any given situation, you have a choice of what to expect.

1. **You can expect the worst** – Many people are living their lives as perpetual victims. Everything is against them and no matter how hard they try, they can't succeed. As a result of this defeatist mentality, they simply give up, or give effort with a "what good will it do?" outlook. As a self-fulfilling prophecy to their *devout* negativism, life will only give what is expected. **If you expect the worst, it would be against nature's law of reciprocity to give you the best!**

2. **You can expect nothing** – It would seem strange to think that someone could have <u>no</u> expectation, but there are people who drift through life with no definite aim or purpose. People can drift day to day, *even* with positive outlooks on life, but have no real level of expectation and a **plan for its achievement**. It is hard to know if success has been achieved if there is no preconceived concept of success (expectation). The absence of specific expectations or goals would leave each day to chance and happenstance versus it being a day on purpose with defined targets.

3. **You expect the best** – Certainly, the best type of expectation comes from having a specific plan for a goals achievement. Depending on the source you cite, only 3% - 10% of the population has ***defined goals*** with tactical plans to achieve them. Sure, almost everyone *says* they want to be rich, lose weight, start a business, and enjoy life to the full. Those are essentially empty pipe dreams if not fueled by plans to accomplish them. **You can determine how serious someone is** *(and more importantly, how likely they are to achieve their goals)* **if they have written defined plans**. There is supreme power to expecting the best, making

plans for those expectations, and living each day as if "Today is going to be the day!"

Establishing Initial Expectations For Your Life

When you ask most people *who* they want to be in life, they are unsure of their mission, or calling. But if you ask people *what* they want, they are more apt to be able to tell you. The kind of car, the home, the clothes, and all the outward material elements of their vision of successful life are usually easier to express than their life's purpose. This is due in large part to advertising from Madison Avenue. We are bombarded 24/7 with symbols of status and the trappings of success on every hand but there is little guidance as it relates to **who we must become to obtain these things.**

Understand that the desire for material possession is inherent to your makeup and material possessions can actually be a demonstration of the equitable exchange of value you provide to others who **need** your unique gifts. Yes, some of us are driven more by status than service, but when you "flow in your gift" each good material thing you manifest feels like a reward for a life well lived and not a validation of your importance or status.

What is your calling or purpose that can help you live the "good life"? Napoleon Hill in **Think and Grow Rich** calls this your "definite purpose in life". What drives you to get out of bed each day and keeps you up late at night? If you don't know yet *don't worry,* it will become more evident over the next 7 days. If you are unsure of your specific definite purpose, then using your material desires to set your expectation could be the key to discovering it. In tonight's exercises, we will use the simple desire for a new car to create the "Possible Future". **That focus on material desire could be the key to help you unlock the "hidden gifts" that will help you manifest that possible future!**

The Power of Desire!

"Where there is no vision, people perish" - *Proverbs 29:19*. Vision is the force that keeps us alive and pushes us into becoming the creation that providence intended. The reward of fulfilling that destiny is every desire that we could ever dream or hope for. It is a bonus for living life on the highest level. **There is inside of you, right now, <u>all</u> the talents and abilities to manifest this and greater good.** The inherent and programmed desire for material things is not evil, if we use our greatest gifts in service to mankind as the means to achieve them. We get out of line when the desire for material things drives us to act foolishly - high debt, envy, jealousy, and corruption.

In the simplistic translation De Sire means "of the father" or "from the king". All desire comes from a seed of promise you received at birth and tugs at the deepest part of your soul and spirit to beckon you to your destiny. This statement is not about doctrine or which religion you subscribe to. These internal promptings and compulsions are part of your DNA and operate on you "involuntarily', **just like your heartbeat**...it doesn't need your permission or approval to summon you to your gift...*it simply does*. <u>**If this grand plan for your life is followed, the things that you so greatly yearn for will be yours.**</u>

While some of the things you desire may seem out of reach or too far-fetched, desire is in a **one to one** ratio with the ability to achieve it! You will not be given Mercedes Benz desire and only be given "clunker" ability! Many people have inherent fear that goes along with their desires, or the pursuit of their calling. That is the key to expanding and evolving life...to understand that the best desires come *"gift wrapped"* in <u>doubt and fear</u>, but once you tear off the packaging, <u>**all**</u> is yours to enjoy!

That fear and doubt, when it comes, is not designed to rob you of your desires, but to throw you off track from the optimal plan of how to acquire them. Fundamentally, it is not the attainment of material things that brings happiness and fulfillment - it is **what we do and who we become,** to obtain them that brings happiness. There are many people using "developed" gifts to obtain cars, houses, and build a large net worth, but they are not fulfilled in their daily work because they are not using their "natural gifts". This avocation is funding their material lifestyle but they are spiritually "bankrupt".

You may fear your ability to "disconnect" from this subtle form of slavery (Golden Handcuffs is more politically correct), but to redirect your life and begin pursuing your **True Vocation** is the beginning of the "Pursuit of Happiness". Fear and doubt are natural. You may fear and doubt your ability to accomplish what appears, today, to be lofty goals. Realize that in all that you are compelled to do, and for all the good that waits for *your excellence*, there is only one thing that is consistently required of you – **BE STRONG AND OF A GOOD COURAGE!**

I am reminded of a high school cheer that my sister (the really popular, pretty cheerleader and homecoming queen - no envy - *really!*) used to do at football games. While it dates back to the 70's, it is quite appropriate for this moment. It simply said, "*Elevate Your Mind, Get Yourself Together*". The powerful phrase was repeated in various rhythmic patterns until the crowd was worked up for the home team. Remind yourself, everyday, that you (via your mind) are in control of your life!

Elevate Your Mind, Get Yourself Together!

Excercise #1 - Sample
A Measure of Success - *What Do You Expect?*

You are *"Here"*	You want to be *"There"*
The following series of exercises will help determine where you are today with the Fab Five. They will help define a potential Mental Sticking Point (M.S.P) of limitation in each area.	Once you have determined where you are, each exercise gives you the opportunity to state where you *want to be*. Don't focus on **How** you will get "There" yet...for now, we are examining *your expectations* of what is possible in your life.

Financially

For **Your Employment Status** and **How Much You Earn**, put a "here" for your present status and a "there" for where you can see yourself in the future.

Your Employment Status

Unemployed	Employee	Management	VP	CEO	Self-Employed
		Here			*There*

How Much You Earn

<$25,000	$25,000 - $50,000	$50,000 - $75,000	$75,000 – $100,000	$100,000 - $500,000	$500,000 - $1,000,000	>$1,000,000
		Here		*There*		

Your Net Worth

For each question below, simply answer "yes" or "no" based on each specific amount listed. The first row that has all "no's" represents your perceived "max".

Amounts	Have Now?	Had Before?	Get In Future?	1 Year?	5 years?	10 Years?	Lifetime ?
$100	Yes	Yes	Yes	Yes	Yes	Yes	Yes
$1,000	Yes	Yes	Yes	Yes	Yes	Yes	Yes
$10,000	Yes	Yes	Yes	Yes	Yes		es
$100,000	No	No	Yes	No	Yes	M.S.P is	es
$500,000	No	Yes	Yes	No	Yes	$10,000,000	es
$1,000,000	No	No	Yes	No	No	Yes	Yes
$10,000,000	No	No	No	No	No	No	No
$50,000,000	No	No	No	No	No	No	No
$100,000,000	No	No	No	No	No	No	No
$1,000,000,000	No	No	No	No	No	No	No

Spiritually

Do you feel connected to your inner spirit and at peace with yourself as a person?

Never	Sometimes	Most of the time	Always
	Here		*There*

If you are part of an organized religion, how active and involved are you?

Never	Seldom	Occasionally	As I am called	Always
		Here	*There*	

Mentally

How would you describe your outlook on life and the possibilities it presents?

Cynicism	Pessimism	Realism	Optimism
	Here		There

How much time and energy do you spend on self-development and improvement?

Never	Seldom	Occasionally	Frequently	Always
		Here		There

On a scale of 1-10, how would you rate your happiness and fulfillment?

1	2	3	4	5	6	7	8	9	10
				Here				There	

Physically

For **Your Weight, Physical Condition** and **Total Image**, put a "here" for your present status and a "there" for where you can see yourself in the future.

-25lbs +	-15-24lbs	-1-14lbs	Perfect Weight!	1-14lbs	15-24lbs	25lbs +
			There		Here	

Physical Condition

Chronically Ill	Poor Health	Fair Health	Good Health	Perfect Health!
			Here	There

Total Image

1	2	3	4	5	6	7	8	9	10
				Here				There	

Socially

How much do you interact with others socially?

Recluse	Work Only	Family Only	Socially Active	Facebook addict
	Here		There	

How many friendly acquaintances do you have outside of work?

1-5	5-10	15-20	25-30	30+
Here			There	

How many people would you call a close friend?

1	2	3	4	5+
Here	There			

On a scale of 1-10, how would you rate your relationship with your spouse/significant other?

1	2	3	4	5	6	7	8	9	10
						Here		There	

On a scale of 1-10, how would you rate your relationships with your children/immediate family?

1	2	3	4	5	6	7	8	9	10
						Here		There	

Exercise #1
A Measure of Success - *What Do You Expect?*
Financially

For **Your Employment Status** and **How Much You Earn**, put a "here" for your present status and a "there" for where you can see yourself in the future.

Your Employment Status					
Unemployed	Employee	Management	VP	CEO	Self-Employed

How Much You Earn						
<$25,000	$25,000 - $50,000	$50,000 - $75,000	$75,000 – $100,000	$100,000 - $500,000	$500,000 - $1,000,000	>$1,000,000

Your Net Worth

For each question below, simply answer "yes" or "no" based on each specific amount listed. The first row that has all "no's" represents your perceived "max".

Amounts	Have Now?	Had Before?	Get In Future?	1 Year?	5 years?	10 Years?	Lifetime ?
$100							
$1,000							
$10,000							
$100,000							
$500,000							
$1,000,000							
$10,000,000							
$50,000,000							
$100,000,000							
$1,000,000,000							

Spiritually

Do you feel connected to your inner spirit and at peace with yourself as a person?

Never	Sometimes	Most of the time	Always

If you are part of an organized religion, how active and involved are you?

Never	Seldom	Occasionally	As I am called	Always

Mentally

How would you describe your outlook on life and the possibilities it presents?

Cynicism	Pessimism	Realism	Optimism

How much time and energy do you spend on self-development and improvement?

Never	Seldom	Occasionally	Frequently	Always

On a scale of 1-10, how would you rate your happiness and fulfillment?									
1	2	3	4	5	6	7	8	9	10

Physically

For **Your Weight, Physical Condition** and **Total Image**, put a "here" for your present status and a "there" for where you can see yourself in the future.

-25lbs +	-15-24lbs	-1-14lbs	Perfect Weight!	1-14lbs	15-24lbs	25lbs +

Physical Condition

Chronically Ill	Poor Health	Fair Health	Good Health	Perfect Health!

Total Image

1	2	3	4	5	6	7	8	9	10

Socially

How much do you interact with others socially?

Recluse	Work Only	Family Only	Socially Active	Facebook addict

How many friendly acquaintances do you have outside of work?

1-5	5-10	15-20	25-30	30+

How many people would you call a close friend?

1	2	3	4	5+

On a scale of 1-10, how would you rate your relationship with your spouse/significant other?

1	2	3	4	5	6	7	8	9	10

On a scale of 1-10, how would you rate your relationships with your children and immediate family?

1	2	3	4	5	6	7	8	9	10

Exercise #2 - Sample
What Drives You? *The Possible Future!*

Step #1	Step #3	Step #5
Choose the car(s) of your dreams - Suspend all thoughts of limitation!	Multiply the total value of the cars by two (X 2)...this is your possible income.	Multiply the value of your homes by four (X 4)...this is your net worth in the next 5-10 years.
Step #2	**Step #4**	
Calculate the total costs of the cars desired	Multiply your income by 3 (x 3)...this is the value of your home(s)	

		Year	Make	Model	Cost
The Cars of Your Dreams	Car 1	2011	BMW	745	$85,000
	Car 2	2011	R. Rover	Sport	$70,000
	Car 3	2011	Chevrolet	Corvette	$55,000
			Total Cost		**$210,000**

Multiply x 2

Earning Potential	**Car Total**		**Your *Immediate* Earning Potential**
	$210,000	X 2 =	*$420,000*

Multiply x 3

Homes Value	**Earning Potential**		**Your Home(s)**
	$420,000	X 3 =	*$1,260,000*

Multiply x 4

Net Worth	**Home(s) Value**		**Your Net Worth In 5 – 10 Years**
	$1,260,000	X 4 =	***$5,040,000***

Exercise #2

What Drives You? *The Possible Future!*

		Year	Make	Model	Cost
The Cars of Your Dreams	Car 1				
	Car 2				
	Car 3				
	Total Cost				

Multiply x 2

Earning Potential	**Car Total**		**Your *Immediate* Earning Potential**
		X 2 =	

Multiply x 3

Homes Value	**Earning Potential**		**Your Home(s)**
		X 3 =	

Multiply x 4

Net Worth	**Home(s) Value**		**Your Net Worth In 5 – 10 Years**
		X 4 =	

Exercise #3 - Sample
The Possible Future – *Visualization!*

Find a quiet spot to relax, preferably lying down in a dark room. Begin by focusing on the cars you desire, imagining yourself behind the wheel with as much detail as possible. Start slowly to include the other material elements of this vision. _Emotionalize_ the feelings with as vivid an image as you can develop. Don't be discouraged, this can take concentration and "letting go" on your part. Do not be concerned in the least "how" this will happen, only see it manifested! After 10 minutes of meditation, journal your "inner findings" based on the following questions.

Starting Point		Multiply x 2		Multiply x 3		Multiply x 4	
	Cars		Income		Home(s)		Net Worth
	$210,000		$420,000		$1,260,000		$5,040,000

What Were Your Thoughts During the "Show"?

It was awkard at fist, trying to see myself with all these material desires, but I could feel a pull of desire as the glimpses faded in and out of focus. There was a feeling of being overwhelmed and excited at the same time, not knowing how I would achieve this vision, but that I knew I wanted to! For the first time, I felt I COULD DO IT!!!

How Would You Feel If This Vision Became Reality?

If this vision came to pass, I would feel terrific and fulfilled!!! I would feel as if I had accomplished something major and great, and that I was making the most of my life.

What Stops You Today From Pursuing This Vision?

I realize that there is so much potential that I am not maximizing in my life. My use of time, talents or simply, procrastination and doubt are keeping me from pursuing more. I have no real idea how I can achieve such lofty goals. I have been let down by dreams before and I don't want the pain of failure if I fall short - excuses!!!

9 Gut Check Questions

		Yes	No
1.	Would you be fulfilled if this vision became true?	✓	
2.	Do you believe that you deserve this kind of life?	✓	
3.	Do you think you could develop a plan to live this life?	✓	
4.	Is this vision already in motion?		✓
5.	Are you aware of others living this kind of life?	✓	
6.	Do you believe you have the ability to live this?	✓	
7.	Are you currently maximizing your gifts and ability?		✓
8.	Do you have a written, organized plan?		✓
9.	Are you committed to doing what it takes to live this life?	✓	

6 "Yes" Answers!

How Did You Score? (Number of Questions Answered With "Yes")

0-2	3-5	6-8	All 9
Hang in there!	On your way!	Matter of time!	Inevitable!

Exercise #3
The Possible Future – *Visualization!*

Starting Point $		Multiply x 2	Cars $	Multiply x 3	Income $	Multiply x 4	Home(s) $	Net Worth $

What Were Your Thoughts During the "Show"?

How Would You Feel If This Vision Became Reality?

What Stops You Today From Pursuing This Vision?

9 Gut Check Questions

		Yes	No
1.	Would you be fulfilled if this vision became true?		
2.	Do you believe that you deserve this kind of life?		
3.	Do you think you could develop a plan to live this life?		
4.	Is this vision already in motion?		
5.	Are you aware of others living this kind of life?		
6.	Do you believe you have the ability to live this life?		
7.	Are you currently maximizing your gifts and ability?		
8.	Do you have a written, organized plan?		
9.	Are you committed to doing what it takes to live this life?		

How Did You Score? (Number of Questions Answered With "Yes")

0-2	3-5	6-8	All 9
Hang in there!	On your way!	Matter of time!	Inevitable!

JOURNAL, NOTES AND KEY LEARNINGS

You. *Change.* Now!

_____

_____

_____

_____

_____

_____

_____

_____

_____

_____

_____

_____

_____

_____

_____

_____

_____

_____

_____

_____

_____

_____

_____

_____

_____

_____

_____

DAY 1 - ELEVATE YOUR MIND

_____

_____

_____

_____

_____

_____

_____

_____

_____

_____

_____

_____

_____

_____

_____

_____

_____

_____

_____

_____

_____

_____

_____

Congratulations on completing Day 1! Here are Free resources available with this book:

Visit You. *Change*. Now! FREE Resources page by inserting this information into your browser;

http://www.brandonlclay.com/#!ycn-resouce-center/c1z1u

If you need assistance with these resources email: bclay@brandonlclay.com

Bonus #1 -
Workshops & Journal Pages!
You will find PDF's (larger 8 ½ x 11) of all the life changing workshops and exercises that can be printed out each day as you complete the written material!

Bonus #2 -

Complete Audio reading of You. *Change*. Now! By Brandon L Clay!
This convenient format allows you to reinforce your learnings in the car, at the gym…all from your MP3 device!

Day Two - Activate the Triune Mind

Whatever we plant in our subconscious mind and nourish with repetition and emotion will one day become a reality.
Earl Nightingale

As you can see from the first day's sessions and exercises, **the mind is a powerful tool**. It is an incredible time machine that can propel us into the future, recreate a painful or pleasurable past, and give us all the sensations as if it were real today! The apparatus that allows us to create a compelling future and sensualize it in the "here and now" is the **Triune Mind**. Don't allow the fancy, scientific terminology to faze you...thankfully, we all have one and use it daily, whether we know it or not. The Triune Mind is made up of three components:

- **Conscious**
- **Sub-conscious**
- **Super-conscious**

The **conscious mind** is driven by the five physical senses of taste, touch, sound, smell and sight. For most, the conscious mind is the dominant judgment system utilized for determining what is possible in their lives. It is limited in that it can only process information that is presented through the five physical senses. It cannot think "out of the box". It only knows "What" it wants and needs based on the five physical senses. It requires assistance from the sub-conscious mind to see beyond the obvious.

The **sub-conscious mind** has the ability to propel you into the future. It supports the conscious mind by giving it the reasons to take an action and the likelihood that the actions will manifest the desired results – *thus eliminating fear*, or at least creating a mindset conducive for action. Of course, it can just as easily do the opposite and **create fear** based on conclusions it makes from the data supplied by the conscious mind. It can create *unlimited* images vividly with consistency and it is these meditated "realities" that will drive or inhibit action. **The sub-conscious mind does not understand whether a thought is truly real or only imagined.** It creates the "Why" emotions that drive the conscious mind into action, if presented passionately enough.

The **super-conscious mind** delivers the "How" answers based on "What" the conscious mind wants and "Why" the sub-conscious mind says we want it. It is the direct contact with the Universal Mind, though it is called by many names. *It* provides the roadmap with clarity and focus. **It provides answers to complex issues in direct proportion to the attention and trust that is given to it.** It will integrate seamlessly with our abilities to resolve problems and achieve desired outcomes - thus helping us to achieve more than we think is possible.

These three together form the **Triune Mind**...*the conscious, sub-conscious and super-conscious.* When used properly, they create a powerful trio that can propel you to success in *any* area of your life and will help **You.** *Change.* **Now!**

Mixing the What, Why & How Cocktail

To understand how the Triune Mind works we must understand the responsibility of each component. The conscious mind is responsible for **"What"** – the wish list of life. The sub-conscious mind creates the **"Why"** – the strong and compelling emotional reasons these desires are important. Finally, the super-conscious delivers the **"How"** – the specific strategies to obtain the things highly desired.

Of course, not everyone engages the super-conscious to get the optimal strategies for obtaining what they desire. The result will be strategies that may help them obtain **what** they desire but have residual consequences. These negative and potentially destructive strategies come from not engaging and trusting the super-conscious for direction. As a result, people will do *consciously* driven activity to obtain those things they desire. Some will resort to getting themselves into excessive debt, or they will get involved in unlawful activity to obtain their desires.

In order to keep the three in balance, **the conscious mind must focus on what it wants, the subconscious mind must allow us to feel its attainment, and the super-conscious mind must be trusted to deliver how we will obtain it.** *The three minds must act as one mind.* All three are equally important if we are to achieve Money, Power and Success and greatness in our lives!

What? – The Fab Five

To live a full life, you need to determine what you desire in the Fab Five – Financially, Mentally, Spiritually, Physically and Socially. The Triune Mind will demand balance in your life. Some people will place more importance on financial things, but your spirit might suffer if this focus is out of balance. To some, living a high social life may be a priority, but their physical health suffers as a result. Activating the Triune Mind will develop success in each area. You will realize that you can have **complete success** and no area has to be neglected. Our goal setting exercises will delve into each of the Fab Five to create a holistic and complete vision for your life...one that is not lacking in any area! Goals require several components to be effective:

- Measurable
- Challenging but not unrealistic
- Consistent with your highest and best abilities
- Time bound with deadlines for achievement
- Flexible
- Reviewed Frequently

The goal setting exercises will guide you to ensure each of your desires meets these criteria. In order to get the most out of the Triune Mind, we must go against our nature and prove to ourselves that we are serious about our intent **to act** on what we desire. It is not enough to *say* what we want, **we must write it down**. There is a magic in the written word. Remember Yul Brenner in The Ten Commandments, "*So let it be written, so let it be done*"?

Write the vision and make it so specific that the reader (you!) will be inspired to achieve it. If consistently written, reviewed, and visualized it will eventually manifest! Most people do not have written defined goals that drive and motivate them to greater achievement. Taking the time to write your goals demonstrates to your sub-conscious and the super-conscious mind that you are serious about your life. **It also tells the sub-conscious what to dream about and focus on, giving the super-conscious mind a "mandate" to provide an answer.**

Why? – The Compelling Reasons That Create Action

Why do you want the things you desire? There are five major emotions that drive us toward our goals and dreams – **fulfillment, pleasure, achievement, security, and independence**. There are many other names for our driving emotions but they will correspond to one of these. Think of the reasons that you would like these things in your life and how receiving them will impact your life!

The power of "why" is a key driving force behind the achievement of any desire. It determines our **level of expectation**, which we have learned, determines our outcomes. "Why" can be based on desperation or inspiration. People are typically motivated by the carrot or the stick. *When will a child run faster? When running toward the ice cream truck, or running from a big dog?* Certainly, positive inducements create the best kind of motivation but the majority of people never take the time to create these positive "why" emotions. They are driven episodically by deadlines, ultimatums, and "do or die" motivation. There is a better way!

Powerful emotional words create the positive imagery that is required to move the hand of the super-conscious mind to provide answers and lead us to the resources we need. Fearful imagery (desperation) will hinder the process and make you subject to fear and inaction. Emotion gives your vision graphic color and a vivid appearance that sends a consistent message to the super-conscious. Delivering a vivid, consistent and focused "why" gives the super-conscious the "bridge" it needs to send you the "How". Consistent, vivid imaginings also activates several laws:

1. **The Law of Attraction** - In recent years, the law of attraction has gained much popularity as a principle of achievement. Its core concept is that we draw to us what we focus on and that "As a man thinketh in his heart, so is he". **As you flood your mind with desire and outcomes, you create a magnetic energy that brings these desires to you.** The imagination is key to this law in that you must believe that you have received these things even *before* their physical appearance. **Creating compelling "why's" and engaging the subconscious mind is the only way to create this white heat of desire and belief - thus magnetizing you to your obectives.**

2. **The Law of Reciprocity -** In a world of supply and demand, something must be given before anything can be received. To get goods, services or money something of equitable value must be exchanged. To get stronger physically, we must give what we have physically (exercise) as part of that transaction. Sowing must be done *before* there is reaping. **All initial "seeds" will be seeds of thought.** As the Law of Reciprocity is set in motion, these "thought seeds' will grow into our destiny.

3. **The Law of Perfect Action** - One of the benefits of an active imagination is mapping out strategies and tactics toward the attainment of the thing imagined. The more vivid and consistent the

image, the more resolute the action necessary to obtain it becomes. Great inventors, such as Tesla, spent countless hours in imagining the construction of their inventions *before* pursuing them in the laboratory. This reliance on activating the Triune Mind, eliminated much of the trial and error of the inventive process and delivered a "divine strategy" from the super-conscious mind with regularity...**and with stunning results!**

4. **The Law of Habit** - The greatest achievers in history were not creatures of happenstance or given to procrastination. They were so driven by their desires that the actions necessary for achievement were not left to fate. They became their dreams and desires. This higher state of being generates a series of *automatic actions*...**habits** that sustained them until their goals were manifested. As you create vivid and consistent images of your desires, the compelling "why" emotions will spur you to action, and these actions will eventually become "*first nature*"...habits. This new found discipline will make all you desire not only possible, but inevitable!

5. **The Law of Fear Elimination** - Fear is the single greatest enemy to achievement. Out of it is born procrastination, timidity, inaction, and every other destroyer of destiny known to man! As you continue in engaging your **Triune Mind** with focused and regular imaginings, you will remove fear from your thinking as the transmissions of *Perfect Action*, give you confidence in your strategies. The word confidence is built from "*Con*" (with) and "*Fidelity*" (truth)...**once you know the truth, you will be in the highest state of faith and fear will no longer govern your actions.**

Exercise #4A - Sample
Life Transforming Goal Workshop - Let Your Imagination Run *What* Wild!

Step One	Step Two	Step Three
In the Brainstorm section, spend at least 3 minutes on what you desire for each of the Fab Five categories Don't try to figure out how they will happen!	In the Brainstorm section, write when you will achieve each of the goals in the Fab Five Use increments of 6 months, 1 - 3 years, 5 - 10 years, choosing a time that is closest to your expectation	In the *Top Three Goals* section, rank your 3 highest priority goals for each of the Fab Five by time frame of expected achievement

WHAT? FINANCIALLY!

Power Suggestions

- Annual Salary
- Develop and Maintain Budget
- Diversify investment portfolio
- Material Desires
- Chart Career Path
- Start a business
- Be Debt Free
- Buy a Home
- Build Retirement
- Net worth

Brainstorm Financial Goals

Time	Goal	Time	Goal	Time	Goal
6 mo	100k salary	3 yr	200k salary	5 yr	500k salary
1 yr	Invest 10k	10 yr	Beach condo	3 yr	Invest 100k
1 yr	BMW	5 yr	Leave job	10 yr	Millionaire
1 yr	Start business	3 yr	Dream Home	3 yr	Parents 10k yr

Rank Financial Goals

Rank	Short Term	Rank	Intermediate	Rank	Long Term
1	100k salary	1	200k Salary	1	500k Salary
2	Start business	2	Parents 10k yr.	2	Millionaire
3	Invest 10k	3	Invest 100k	3	Leave corp. job
4	BMW	4	Dream home	4	Beach condo

Top Three Financial Goals

Rank	Short Term	Rank	Intermediate	Rank	Long Term
1	100k salary	1	200k salary	1	500k salary
2	Start business	2	Parents 10k yr.	2	Millionaire
3	Invest 10k	3	Invest 100k	3	Beach condo

Exercise #4B - Sample

Life Transforming Goal Workshop - How Hard You Try Is Based On *Why!*

Step One	Step Two	Step Three
Write your top 3 Short-Term, Intermediate, and Long Term goals	From the Power Thesaurus, choose at least 3 words that best describe the feeling you will get from achieving the goal.	Journal your thoughts about *how you will feel* achieving these goals using your Power **Why** words

WHY?

FINANCIALLY!

Power Thesaurus

- Fulfillment – Satisfaction, Gratification, Completion, Accomplishment
- Pleasure – Enjoyment, Happiness, Desire, Privilege
- Achievement – Triumph, Realization, Victory, Attainment
- Security – Confidence, Certainty, Peace of Mind, Faithful
- Independence – Freedom, Liberation, Autonomy, Sovereignty

Rank	Short Term Financial Goals	Key Emotional *WHY* Words
1	100k salary	Fulfillment, Accomplishment, Peace of Mind
2	Start business	Independence, Freedom, Autonomy, Victory
3	Invest 10k	Security, Attainment, Liberation
Rank	Intermediate Financial Goals	Key Emotional *WHY* Words
1	200k salary	Enjoyment, Peace, Desire, Liberation
2	Give parents 10k a year	Pleasure, Realization, Attainment
3	Invest 100k	Security, Attainment, Certainty of Wealth
Rank	Long Term Financial Goals	Key Emotional *WHY* Words
1	500k salary	Independence, Safety, Satisfaction, Peace
2	Millionaire	Pleasure, Enjoyment, Realization, Freedom
3	Beach condo	Happiness, Privilege, Gratification

Emotional *WHY* Journal Entry
Short Term Financial Goals

Achieving my short term financial goals means fulfilling some major objectives in my life. The feeling of accomplishment that realizing these goals gives me is tremendous! To know that I have the ability to earn six figures gives me great confidence and peace of mind for my financial future. Starting my business is the beginning of my independence...freedom from the chains of corporate life.

Intermediate Financial Goals

The ability to earn $200,000 while working for myself is liberating to my mind, and a victory that I have waited a lifetime to celebrate! The freedom and autonomy will allow me to serve countless others, as I share my gifts and abilities. Sharing my blessing of income with my parents and still invest 100k is a privilege and realization of my dreams.

Exercise #4A - Let Your Imagination Run *What* Wild!

WHAT?
FINANCIALLY!

Power Suggestions	
• Annual Salary	• Chart Career Path
• Develop Budget	• Start a business
• Diversify investment portfolio	• Be Debt Free
	• Buy a Home
• Material Desires	• Net worth

Brainstorm Financial Goals

Time	Goal	Time	Goal

Rank	Short Term	Rank	Intermediate	Rank	Long Term
1		1		1	
2		2		2	
3		3		3	

Exercise #4B - How Hard You Try Is Based On *Why!*

	Power Thesaurus
WHY? FINANCIALLY!	• Fulfillment – Satisfaction, Gratification, Completion, Accomplishment • Pleasure – Enjoyment, Happiness, Desire, Privilege • Achievement – Triumph, Realization, Victory, Attainment • Security – Confidence, Certainty, Peace of Mind, Faithful • Independence – Freedom, Liberation, Autonomy, Sovereignty

Rank	Short Term Financial Goals	Key Emotional *WHY* Words

Rank	Intermediate Financial Goals	Key Emotional *WHY* Words

Rank	Long Term Financial Goals	Key Emotional *WHY* Words

Emotional *WHY* Journal Entry
Short Term Financial Goals

Intermediate Financial Goals

Long Term Financial Goals

Exercise #4A - Let Your Imagination Run *What* Wild!

WHAT? SPIRITUALLY!

Power Suggestions	
• Inner Peace and connection • Prayer life • Meditate daily • Relationship with God • Forgive past hurts	• Giving to others • Living stress free • Determining major purpose in life • Community Involvement

Brainstorm Spiritual Goals

Time	Goal	Time	Goal

Rank	Short Term	Rank	Intermediate	Rank	Long Term
1		1		1	
2		2		2	
3		3		3	

Exercise #4B - How Hard You Try Is Based On *Why!*

	Power Thesaurus
WHY? **SPIRITUALLY!**	• Fulfillment – Satisfaction, Gratification, Completion, Accomplishment • Pleasure – Enjoyment, Happiness, Desire, Privilege • Achievement – Triumph, Realization, Victory, Attainment • Security – Confidence, Certainty, Peace of Mind, Faithful • Independence – Freedom, Liberation, Autonomy, Sovereignty

Rank	Short Term Spiritual Goals	Key Emotional *WHY* Words

Rank	Intermediate Spiritual Goals	Key Emotional *WHY* Words

Rank	Long Term Spiritual Goals	Key Emotional *WHY* Words

Emotional *WHY* Journal Entry
Short Term Spiritual Goals

Intermediate Spiritual Goals

Long Term Spiritual Goals

Exercise #4A - Let Your Imagination Run *What* Wild!

WHAT? MENTALLY!	Power Suggestions	
	• Develop Success Attributes • Uncover creative gifts • Keep a personal journal • Obtain a degree	• Read a book a month • Increase memory • Learn a new language • Control thoughts

Brainstorm Mental Goals

Time	Goal	Time	Goal

Rank	Short Term	Rank	Intermediate	Rank	Long Term
1		1		1	
2		2		2	
3		3		3	

Exercise #4B - How Hard You Try Is Based On *Why!*

WHY?
MENTALLY!

Power Thesaurus

- Fulfillment – Satisfaction, Gratification, Completion, Accomplishment
- Pleasure – Enjoyment, Happiness, Desire, Privilege
- Achievement – Triumph, Realization, Victory, Attainment
- Security – Confidence, Certainty, Peace of Mind, Faithful
- Independence – Freedom, Liberation, Autonomy, Sovereignty

Rank	Short Term Mental Goals	Key Emotional *WHY* Words

Rank	Intermediate Mental Goals	Key Emotional *WHY* Words

Rank	Long Term Mental Goals	Key Emotional *WHY* Words

Emotional *WHY* Journal Entry
Short Term Mental Goals

Intermediate Mental Goals

Long Term Mental Goals

Exercise #4A - Let Your Imagination Run *What* Wild!

WHAT? PHYSICALLY!	Power Suggestions	
	• Achieve and maintain ideal weight	• Health eating habits
	• Exercise 3-5 times a week	• Image makeover
	• Aerobic and weight training regime	• Lower cholesterol and blood pressure
	• Better personal hygiene	• Improved sex life
		• Decrease "age"

Brainstorm Physical Goals

Time	Goal	Time	Goal

Rank	Short Term	Rank	Intermediate	Rank	Long Term
1		1		1	
2		2		2	
3		3		3	

Exercise #4B - How Hard You Try Is Based On *Why!*

WHY? PHYSICALLY!	**Power Thesaurus**
	• Fulfillment – Satisfaction, Gratification, Completion, Accomplishment
	• Pleasure – Enjoyment, Happiness, Desire, Privilege
	• Achievement – Triumph, Realization, Victory, Attainment
	• Security – Confidence, Certainty, Peace of Mind, Faithful
	• Independence – Freedom, Liberation, Autonomy, Sovereignty

Rank	Short Term Physical Goals	Key Emotional *WHY* Words

Rank	Intermediate Physical Goals	Key Emotional *WHY* Words

Rank	Long Term Physical Goals	Key Emotional *WHY* Words

Emotional *WHY* Journal Entry
Short Term Physical Goals

Intermediate Physical Goals

Long Term Physical Goals

Exercise #4A - Let Your Imagination Run *What* Wild!

WHAT? SOCIALLY!

Power Suggestions

- Supporting family and friends
- Build business network
- Attend cultural events
- Travel the world

- Be a mentor
- Entertain close friends monthly
- A better relationship with spouse
- Join Toastmasters

Brainstorm Social Goals

Time	Goal	Time	Goal

Rank	Short Term	Rank	Intermediate	Rank	Long Term
1		1		1	
2		2		2	
3		3		3	

Exercise #4B - How Hard You Try Is Based On *Why!*

WHY? SOCIALLY!

Power Thesaurus

- Fulfillment – Satisfaction, Gratification, Completion, Accomplishment
- Pleasure – Enjoyment, Happiness, Desire, Privilege
- Achievement – Triumph, Realization, Victory, Attainment
- Security – Confidence, Certainty, Peace of Mind, Faithful
- Independence – Freedom, Liberation, Autonomy, Sovereignty

Rank	Short Term Social Goals	Key Emotional *WHY* Words

Rank	Intermediate Social Goals	Key Emotional *WHY* Words

Rank	Long Term Social Goals	Key Emotional *WHY* Words

Emotional *WHY* Journal Entry
Short Term Social Goals

Intermediate Social Goals

Long Term Social Goals

JOURNAL, NOTES AND KEY LEARNINGS

_____

_____

_____

_____

_____

_____

_____

_____

_____

_____

_____

_____

_____

_____

_____

_____

_____

_____

_____

_____

_____

_____

_____

_____

_____

Day Three - Strategize

There are risks and costs to a program of action. But they are far less than the long-range risks and costs of comfortable inaction.
John F. Kennedy

For most, creating a wish list of desires and the reasons they want them is easy once they actually *focus* on them. Devising a strategy of "how" they can attain them is more difficult. Many give up or turn to other devices for the attainment of a goal. When people want to lose weight or change physically they may resort to fad diets or cosmetic surgery. To live the high life some will rely on the luck of lotteries, crime, or excessive debt. To provide mental escape people will abuse drugs or food. There will always be consequences to these actions that we don't forsee as we engage in various behaviors to live our desired life.

The super-conscious has the answers we need to obtain true success in our lives. **The amount of trust we place in it delivers us to the right strategy and action.** The ratio of attention and trust given determines the level of our ability to receive what is a *"complete transmission"* from the super-conscious mind. There are several ways of how we can receive strategies of how to obtain our goals and dreams:

1. **Trial and Error** - Many people live in a "hit or miss" world. They have lofty goals and dreams but no defined plans for achievement. They are people of action (a good thing!) but will have many failures before they *stumble* into success. The "success or bust" mentality serves them well as they continue despite setbacks, until success is achieved. *This is one way to succeed, but it is the hardest way.*

2. **Observation** - When it comes to achievement, *"imitation is the sincerest form of flattery"*. Most of us will model what we see others do to achieve the things they have achieved. The libraries are full of examples of people who have done the things we wish to do. They chronicle their lives in such a way as to blaze a trail leaving breadcrumbs for anyone else to follow. Starting a business, creating better relationships, or losing weight…there is no topic that you can't find someone willing to share their recipe of success for you to observe, *and emulate*. Infomercials use graphic testimonials to excite us to buy their products as we observe the results of others who have used these products to seemingly great success. **Observation is available to everyone, regardless of their starting point, or desired ending point.**

3. **Intuition, Inspiration and Revelation** - There are some people who appear to be "guided" and when the *eureka* moment arrives, they are fearless in the pursuit of their desired objective. They may not be able to explain the process or why they are so resolute about an idea or course of action, but once prompted they begin, immediately, to "work their plan". They may not even have the entire strategy mapped, but trust that divine ideas will appear at the precise moment needed. They only need to see the next step and have supreme faith in their actions. Some fortunate people receive a flash of brilliance or a *"complete transmission"* of every element of their idea…the highest form of revelation.

The Question of How

To begin answering the question of "How" you will obtain all your desires, we must first look at a very important person – **You!** There is a specific "you" that you must become to manifest all the things you aspire for in life. **Inside each one of us is a seed of perfect completion** ... *Our true self*. For most, that perfect image is buried deep within what is today a much distorted self-image. Each of us has a divine destiny that can make us whole and entire. At birth, we are impregnated with whom we need to be to serve the world and fulfill ourselves. There is an Evolution to Completion that is fundamental to understanding "how" to get where you want to be. That Evolution to Completion begins with <u>Thoughts</u> and ends with <u>Destiny</u>. It consists of:

Thoughts ~ Words ~ Actions ~ Habits ~ Character ~ Reputation ~ Destiny

The Evolution to Completion

Regardless of your *intent*, there **will be** an Evolution to Completion that determines where you will end up – <u>your destiny</u>. **The things you are thinking about today will determine tomorrow's destiny.** Positive thoughts will lead to a positive completion. Negative thoughts will lead to a negative completion. It is possible to change your course and re-direct your Evolution to Completion to match your goals and desires. You have to determine who you are today and if you are headed toward your perfect completion. If you are off course, then you must direct, or re-direct your Evolution to Completion in the Fab Five areas of your life.

Of the "how's" described earlier, the only one that can bring consistent success and the one that you have complete access to is **Observation**. While you can never eliminate all trial and error, you can learn from the example of people who have come before you and achieved the level of greatness that you desire in each of the Fab Five. This type of modeling can accelerate your journey to completion if used effectively and purposefully.

People who have achieved similar levels of success to what you desire are the most powerful advantage you have in your quest for Money, Power, and Success. Modeling their ***Thoughts to Destiny*** gives you a compass that insures you make it to your perfect completion. Take the best attributes of all the people who represent your Fab Five desires and implement them in your life. You need to take a hard look at your life today, and compare it to the lives of others who have demonstrated an ability to perfectly complete their Evolution to Completion journey.

For most people, change brings discomfort. There is the fear of failure, the fear of the unknown. Most people prefer to travel the path of least resistance. Many people find that being forced into changes sometimes has a good result. Losing a job might force you into starting a business or finding the right career. The onset of a medical condition may prompt you to make dietary changes to lose weight and get into shape. Rather than being pushed into the pool, decide to jump in under your own terms. Create your own C.H.A.O.S to become who you need to become.

C. H. A. O. S - *Changing Habits Affecting OutcomeS*

What do you think when you hear the word chaos? Disorder, frantic, out of control, or constantly changing to denote instability? Whenever change is introduced in your life you go through a pattern of *habit interruption.* You are going along, thinking everything is status quo and then...BAM! It feels as though everything changes in an instant, sending your life spiraling out of control. Realize now, that all change is not bad or a sign of imminent doom. In fact, for things to proceed and move forward **You. *Change.* Now!** is necessary...it is vital. CHAOS is good! CHAOS was designed to help you make the positive changes necessary and doing so in a structured manner. Sounds like a contradiction, but it is not.

Your Evolution to Completion is determined by your *thoughts, words, actions, habits, character, and reputation* and they become the drivers to your *destiny.* In order to get on track, we must create CHAOS in each one of the Fab Five to build the proper habits in our lives. Psychology has proven that new habits can be formed in as little as 18 days, but most of us need about 30 days for something to become part of our *first nature* and our daily life pattern. Remember the Transitive Property of Equality in mathematics? Don't be too impressed...*you know the one...*

If **A=B** *and* **B=C** *then* **A=C**

The same rules apply to the progressive steps in the **Evolution to Completion.** If

Thoughts = Habits *and* **Habits = Destiny** *then* **Thoughts = Destiny**

What You Think Will Become Your Destiny

All thoughts are completely within your control. Negative thoughts are the default mode of life for many people. Negative thoughts may not be able to be destroyed completely, but can be brought into captivity in the mind and replaced with a new pattern of positive thought. **Positive thoughts have to be developed.** Thoughts are a form of visualization. Here is an example of a *negative* thought pattern:

> The **conscious mind** (the five physical senses) gives the **sub-conscious mind** what it believes to be the facts about a given situation. The sub-conscious mind then creates a "movie" (imagination) with an NEGATIVE outcome based on these "facts". The sub-conscious mind then delivers the *"moral of the story"* to the conscious mind. The conscious mind then has the permission **not to act** based on the transmission of failure from the sub-conscious. This then controls what is <u>thought</u> and ultimately ***denies*** destiny. **In this type of negative pattern the super-conscious is not consulted.** *The process is exact opposite when the thoughts are positive.*

Thoughts control what we visualize in our mind. As beings made after the "image" of God we have been given the powerful gift of imagination. The power of imagination creates the blueprint and nothing can be held back once the imagination is involved in a positive manner. *Imagination has the power to take us where our immediate situation tells us we can't go.* **There is no limitation to the imagination and therefore, no limits to what we can accomplish!**

You may be dreaming what you think is an impossible dream. **The universe has given you a unique and specific vision to focus on and manifest.** Even if you are in fear, *initially*, you can create a powerful vision to believe in and one in which to place <u>all</u> of your trust. Your vision has to be so vivid and consistent with positive imagery to create an anchor for your belief. Your vision can't depart from you even when circumstances (the facts as seen by your conscious mind) look bleak! Here are the requirements for visualizations in order for them to be effective:

1. **Focused** - Your visualizations should be based on your goals in the Fab Five areas from our previous exercises. *That is why it is vital that your goals be specific.* The more detail you can provide your sub-conscious, the better. Just saying I want a lot of money, a good husband, or a new car is not good enough. You have to be able to provide the exact details from your written goals so there is no ambiguity or vague half-hearted direction to your sub-conscious. There is no Hocus Pocus…only intense focus!

2. **Vivid** - *Even though you will be creating the images of the future with your <u>sub-conscious mind</u>,* you have to create imagery that is consistent with how the **conscious mind** processes information. For example, if you want a new car, you need to visit the showroom to see the car (sight), get in the car and enjoy that new car aroma (smell), take hold of the wheel (touch), and take a test drive and rev up the engine (sound). When you bombard your sub-conscious mind with these tangible aspects of your goal, it will incorporate them into the visualization and it will magnify and expound on the emotional "why" drivers, creating an intense "movie" that will get your juices flowing. Saturating your

mind with specific details and real world facts can only accelerate your achievement of the desired goal!

3. **Consistent** - Once you have created a powerful vision, it is important to play it often. Treat your vision like a sitcom, better yet a sitcom in syndication…play it over and over and over. There are days when some cable stations play nothing but one show for 24 hours…*a marathon!* I love Seinfeld…I watch it when it runs twice a day on television, I have all the seasons on CD and on my IPod. Even though I can recite the lines with them, I still watch! <u>I never get tired of watching</u>. That is the way to treat your imaginings…play them over and over…*even though you know the script like the back of your hand.* **<u>Aren't you a big enough fan of your own life to take time daily to visualize your success?</u>**

Words Are A Reflection of What You Think

The words you speak are the next component of the Evolution to Completion. **You know yourself by your thoughts, the world gets to know you by your words.** If you continually speak negative fear-filled words, the world will get that image of you. The thoughts you think directly control the words you say – out of the abundance of the thoughts, the mouth speaks. Words tell the world where you are with your thoughts. You cannot speak one thing and do another. If your current pattern is negative, or against who you need to be, <u>then you must empty your word container</u>. You must replace all negative or destructive words with positive ones. Condition your mind (Pavlovian dogs – remember day one?) to accept new spoken representations for your outcomes. Remember it may take 18-30 days for your new habit to become first nature.

Structured words that are spoken consistently are affirmations. Your words will always be "affirmed" regardless of their content *or* intent. The world is full of people who say things they really don't want to happen. *Why?* **Speak only** those things that you desire, and <u>never</u> speak against the desired outcome. Affirmations become structured statements that are repeated constantly and confidently with power! *They* work best when begun with <u>**I Am**</u>! Statements such as I am Healthy, I am Wealthy, I am Happy are *first person* affirmations that convey power and resoluteness. The Triune Mind responds to these positive statements and works on avenues to bring them to pass.

Affirmations are also a form of prayer. The conscious mind gives the sub-conscious mind the facts (the what) around a desired outcome. The sub-conscious mind creates a "movie" with the desired outcome. It then delivers the desired outcome via imaginations back to the conscious mind. The conscious mind then thinks thoughts and speaks words in accordance with the outcome desired for the future. *The super-conscious "hears" the words spoken and "sees" the images portrayed.* Since they are in unison, the super-conscious mind sends answers (the how) to the sub-conscious mind. **<u>The sub-conscious mind then incorporates these spiritually obtained answers into the next showing of the "movie" and the conscious mind receives new instructions on what to do and speak about to bring the desired results.</u>**

Music is a powerful anchor for thoughts and affirmations. What song was your first slow dance in school? If you heard the song now, all the emotions and feelings come back, *right?* The memory can provide sensory connection to the time, the place, the sights, the sounds, and smells. You want to create the same powerful physiological connection to your visualizations, and to your affirmations. Incorporate music into your sessions.

Actions Speak Louder Than Words

<u>Actions speak for themselves!</u> Indeed, you can tell if someone is serious about doing something if they are ***doing something.*** Most people get caught up in daydreaming and only talking about what they want out of life. That's a great start, since words are powerful, but what most people are missing is action! *Most people*

know exactly what it is that they need to do to accomplish their goals in life. **What they leave out - is just to do it!**

As mentioned earlier, the thoughts you think and the words you speak will equal the actions you take. The thoughts must be of sufficient intensity to overcome the boundaries to action, such as fear or procrastination. Your words must support these thoughts or you will send your Triune Mind mixed messages and a double-mined man is unstable in all his ways. If your thoughts and words are right, your actions will be right! Action has many benefits that propel you forward and on your way to grand achievement:

1. **Acid Test of Faith** - Action demonstrates an outward show of your belief in your mission in life, your calling. It truly separates you from those who are *just talking.* Action demonstrates commitment to the goal and objective. The bible says in James 2:20, "Faith without corresponding action is dead". It goes on to say "show me a man who is acting appropriately, and I will show you a man of faith".

2. **Compresses Time** - The pursuit of goals gives super-natural energy to achieve thus giving the feeling of having more time or being more effective with the time you have. There are some people, who through indolence and procrastination, always complain of never having enough time. Then there are others, who use the energy of action to compress the precious commodity of time and get more done in a 24 hour day than others can fathom…they are the achievers!

3. **Turns On the Television** - Action fuels your imagination. When you first begin a series of actions, you are likely to dream of these actions at night, and think of them when you are in the car driving - you will think them all the time. You see yourself in the throws of that activity, *the kind of activity that is supposed to bring success.* Your action

provides electricity or "excitement" to your visualizations. **The more you act, the more vivid and real the imaginations…which lead you to more action**…*see the pattern?*

Habits Are Actions On Automatic Pilot

Certainly, action is powerful, *but* if not done consistently, your actions will not yield the desired results. Action taken consistently equals a habit. *Habits are the highest form of action because they do not require conscious thought to be engaged in — they have become automatic!* For most people, habits are destructive, because they follow the path of least resistance. Smoking is an easier habit to keep than kick. Eating sweets is easier than eating healthy and exercising. Make no mistake, it will take proper habits to achieve your desired outcomes. Turning action into habits has many benefits:

1. **Creates momentum** - Habits are three times more effective than sporadic action. For example, if working out at the gym is a sporadic action, you may only go 3 times a week...every *other* week. While that is better action than not going at all, you will likely not achieve the body of your dreams. But if working out is a **daily habit** that is not subject to the whims of scheduling dilemmas *(you know what I mean!)* then you go 5 days a week without fail. It is a habit. Now, you are making gains weekly and can see the desired outcome…which spurs you to more activity in support of your goal.

2. **Demonstrates High Commitment** - A positive habit is one in which the super-conscious gets involved due to continuity of action and a "devout" commitment to your objective. It provides you with inspiration and revelation…things you may not have noticed in your environment before now "*jump out*" in support of your vision. You begin to truly believe you deserve success and your self-imagery is consistent with your God-given gifts.

3. __Compresses Time__ - Once a habit is formed, there is no longer *conscious* awareness or thought to the activity. So time passes quickly versus if you deemed an activity arduous, making time move more slowly. You even begin to look forward to the opportunity to engage in the beneficial activity.

4. __Locks the Channel__ - While sporadic action turns on the television (visualizations) the signal may still be fuzzy due to inconsistency. There is likely an influential book gathering dust on the shelf, or an unused piece of exercise equipment in the basement that hasn't seen use since you paid for it. Habits "hard wire" you into the proper station for your visualizations with a connection that cannot be distorted. __Habits demonstrate and create supreme focus!__

C.H.A.O.S - Putting It All Together

Here is a quick review of all the Evolution to Completion components that we have covered thus far- **Thoughts to Words to Actions to Habits.** These four components are the key drivers to your Self-Image. They create, change, and support the image you have of yourself. This inner representation is then reflected to the world, which responds to you in direct correlation to your own thoughts about yourself. That creates your reputation and that, of course, creates your destiny. Remember, the seed of that entire process is your thoughts!

Using the C.H.A.O.S method empowers you with the abilities necessary to create the proper image to yourself and, ultimately, to the world. Self-image takes time to change, but the possibilities and results will amaze you! When **You. Change. Now!** nothing will be out of your reach!

Exercise #5 - Sample
A Better *WHO* is HOW!

Self-reflection is the first step to start moving in the direction of the goals you have just established. An evaluation of your *current* **thoughts, words, actions, habits, character, reputation, and destiny** will give you a sense of where you are heading.

This exercise is not designed to embarrass you, but enlighten you, so be honest about where you are today...

For each of the Fab Five write a simple sentence that describes the person you are today:

• **Thoughts** - What do you spend most of your time thinking about in each area? Do you think of them at all? Are your current thoughts positive or negative?

• **Words** - What comes out of your mouth on a consistent basis in each area? Do you think of them at all? Are your current words positive or negative?

• **Actions** - What activities do you engage in each area? Are there any activities? Are your current actions constructive or destructive?

• **Habits** - What actions are **automatic** in your life? Do you procrastinate important decisions or actions? Are you consistent or sporadic with critical actions?

• **Character** - What do you *really* think of yourself in each area?

• **Reputation** - What do others really think of you in this area?

• **Destiny** - Based on the answers to all of the above, can you achieve your desired goals with You. Change. Now! ?

HOW?
REFLECTION!

Thoughts	What are you thinking?
Words	What are you saying?
Actions	What are you doing?
Habits	What is automatic?
Character	What do you think about yourself?
Reputation	What do others think about you?
Destiny	Can you get there from here?

Regarding Your Financial Goals - *Where are you right now?*

Thoughts	I am lacking in self-confidence in my ability to earn six figures.
Words	I complain to my friends about how slow I am progressing.
Actions	I have not completed my business plan, nor done any research.
Habits	I haven't consistently invested my "extra" income as I planned.
Character	I know that I have gifts, but I am not sure how to use them best.
Reputation	My last performance appraisal said I was "underachieving".
Destiny	I will not achieve my financial goals if I don't change and focus!

Regarding Your Spiritual Goals - *Where are you right now?*

Thoughts	I only think of spirituality on Sundays and special holidays.
Words	I sometimes gossip with friends and talk negatively about others.
Actions	I do not spend much time meditating, reflecting, or in prayer.
Habits	I have no routine in spending time with myself or God.
Character	I am immature spiritually, and need be true to myself.
Reputation	Unfortunately, I fit in with my friends who influence my choices.
Destiny	I cannot be the person I desire, spiritually, without great change!

Exercise #5 - A Better *WHO* is HOW!

Thoughts	What are you thinking?
Words	What are you saying?
Actions	What are you doing?
Habits	What is automatic?
Character	What do you think about yourself?
Reputation	What do others think about you?
Destiny	Can you get there from here?

Regarding Your Financial Goals - *Where are you right now?*

Thoughts	
Words	
Actions	
Habits	
Character	
Reputation	
Destiny	

Regarding Your Spiritual Goals - *Where are you right now?*

Thoughts	
Words	
Actions	
Habits	
Character	
Reputation	
Destiny	

Regarding Your Mental Goals - *Where are you right now?*	
Thoughts	
Words	
Actions	
Habits	
Character	
Reputation	
Destiny	

Regarding Your Physical Goals - *Where are you right now?*	
Thoughts	
Words	
Actions	
Habits	
Character	
Reputation	
Destiny	

Regarding Your Social Goals - *Where are you right now?*	
Thoughts	
Words	
Actions	
Habits	
Character	
Reputation	
Destiny	

Exercise #6 - Sample
To Be Great ... *Imitate!*

Modeling is the single greatest way to accelerate the achievement of your goals. An evaluation of the **thoughts, words, actions, habits, character, reputation, and destiny** of someone who has achieved the level of success *you* desire gives you a powerful reference point for your own life .

For each of the Fab Five, choose a Role Model.

What was the evolution of their lives from **thought to destiny**? Develop the answers based on how you think that person would respond. Read/Watch their biography, research them on the internet (YouTube is fabulous for live footage research!) to get insight to how they are in each area.

If you don't have access to direct information, then *imagine* how they would answer the questions of how they think, speak, and act.

The key to this exercise is not "hero worship" but to build in your mind a *transformational mental model* of what it takes to duplicate the success of your role model in each area. Of course, your role model will not be perfect! For example, your financial role model may be a billionaire, but physically, they may have health problems or be overweight.

Find a different person in each of the Fab Five areas to ensure you get the best of all worlds.

HOW! **OBSERVATION!**	Thoughts	What do they think?
	Words	What are they saying?
	Actions	What are they doing?
	Habits	What are their habits?
	Character	What do you think about them?
	Reputation	What do others think about them?
	Destiny	Can you get there from here?

Who Is Your *Financial* Role Model?

Thoughts	*I know that he fought poverty by flooding his mind with wealth*
Words	*He recited affirmations daily about his power to get wealth.*
Actions	*He studied investing by going to public library to read newspapers.*
Habits	*Each day he spent 1 hour working on his plans to build a fortune.*
Character	*Despite his surroundings, his self-image was one of success/wealth.*
Reputation	*Known as a hard worker with an uncanny "knack" for investing.*
Destiny	*Became a millionaire at age 26 and billionaire at age 50!*

Exercise #6 - To Be Great ... *Imitate!*

HOW!
OBSERVATION!

Thoughts	What do they think?
Words	What are they saying?
Actions	What are they doing?
Habits	What are their habits?
Character	What do you think about them?
Reputation	What do others think about them?
Destiny	Can you get there from here?

Who Is Your *Financial* Role Model?

Thoughts	
Words	
Actions	
Habits	
Character	
Reputation	
Destiny	

Who Is Your *Spiritual* Role Model?

Thoughts	
Words	
Actions	
Habits	
Character	
Reputation	
Destiny	

Who Is Your *Mental* Role Model?	
Thoughts	
Words	
Actions	
Habits	
Character	
Reputation	
Destiny	

Who Is Your *Physical* Role Model?	
Thoughts	
Words	
Actions	
Habits	
Character	
Reputation	
Destiny	

Who Is Your *Social* Role Model?	
Thoughts	
Words	
Actions	
Habits	
Character	
Reputation	
Destiny	

Exercise #7 - Sample
Visualization Will Lead To Realization!

Dominating thoughts in your life determine what you will become, and what you will achieve in this life. Thoughts are the seeds of life that will...no rather, **must**, reproduce after their kind.

The first step in **C.H.A.O.S** (Changing Habits Affecting OutcomeS) is for You. Change. Now! what you think.

- Using your Role Model, create a series of new thoughts that you need to focus on consistently, based on how you learned they think from the previous exercise.
- Transpose your new *thought statements* to 5 note cards and carry them at all times as reminders whenever your thoughts go back to their "default mode".
- For each area, choose a *memorable* song that you can listen to in the car, on the treadmill, or bedside, that will allow you to create emotional images of your new thoughts and their corresponding achievement.
- Commit to this visualization technique for at least 15 minutes a day (to and from work is ideal!) until the new thought seeds begin to "take root"...and they will!!!

Thoughts	*What do you need to think?*
Words	What do you need to say?
Actions	What do you need to do?
Habits	What needs to be automatic?
Character	What will you think of you?
Reputation	What will others think of you?
Destiny	Will that get you there?

What Do You Need To Think *Financially*?

1,000's of millionaires are created every year, and I have the gifts/talents and the <u>right</u> to be one of them! I am a tremendous business person, and I have valuable ideas and services that I can offer to people and justly charge appropriate value (money) for that exchange. I am generous and helpful to all that need it, especially my parents, who have sacrificed for me to have opportunities in life. I am a wise and successful investor, who makes the right decisions, even after occasional setbacks. I see myself as deserving and capable of achieving great success!!!

Exercise #7 - Visualization Will Lead To Realization!

Step 1   **C.H.A.O.S - Changing Habits Affecting OutcomeS**

Thoughts	*What do you need to think?*
Words	What do you need to say?
Actions	What do you need to do?
Habits	What needs to be automatic?
Character	What will you think of you?
Reputation	What will others think of you?
Destiny	Will that get you there?

What Do You Need To Think *Financially*?

What Do You Need To Think *Spiritually*?

What Do You Need To Think *Mentally*?

What Do You Need To Think *Physically*?

What Do You Need To Think *Socially*?

You. *Change.* Now!

Exercise #8 - Sample
Affirmations Will Bring About Confirmations!

Words are the containers of what we think about on a *consistent basis*. They represent, without fail, to the world, where we are with our thoughts. **Words can inspire action**, and therefore are the truest indicator of *if* we will achieve success in any area of our lives.

The second step in C.H.A.O.S (Changing Habits Affecting OutcomeS) is You. Change. Now! what you say using **affirmations**. An affirmation is simply a group of words that relect a "present tense" positive view of your world and its possibilities.

- Using your role model, create at least 5 affirmations (1 for each area of the Fab Five)
- Transpose your affirmations to 5 note cards.
- Do your best to read/recite these affirmations often during the day...when you wake up and before you go to sleep.

Thoughts	What do you need to think?
Words	*What do you need to say?*
Actions	What do you need to do?
Habits	What needs to be automatic?
Character	What will you think of you?
Reputation	What will others think of you?
Destiny	Will that get you there?

What Do You Need To Say *Financially?*

Money, Money, Money, comes to me from all directions and divine insight.

I have all the skills and abilities necessary to earn the amount of money I desire and need in my life.

All actions that are necessary to achieve my financial goals will be taken by me with NO FEAR!!!

I have the proper relationship with money and giving generously to others is my nature.

I give thanks for all my current financial blessings and look forward to being the steward of even more.

Regardless of the economic conditions, I can evaluate and identify the opportunities that exist and make the most of them.

I have the power to get wealth and to live a life of joy, fulfillment and balance.

Exercise #8 - Affirmations Will Bring About Confirmations!

| Step 2 | C.H.A.O.S - Changing Habits Affecting OutcomeS |

HOW?
AFFIRMATIONS!

Thoughts	What do you need to think?
Words	*What do you need to say?*
Actions	What do you need to do?
Habits	What needs to be automatic?
Character	What will you think of you?
Reputation	What will others think of you?
Destiny	Will that get you there?

What Do You Need To Say *Financially*?

What Do You Need To Say *Spiritually*?

What Do You Need To Say *Mentally?*

What Do You Need To Say *Physically?*

What Do You Need To Say *Socially?*

Exercise #9 - Sample

Action/Habits Make Success Automatic!

Action is the culmination of the thoughts you think and the corresponding words you apply consistently. Action alone is not enough. You must create a lifestyle and not just a series of arduous "*Things To Do Lists*".

You must create the **mindset** that important activities are your 1st *Nature*, so you are not susceptible to procrastination, doubts and fears. **Habits that sustain action and create momentum are the secret of the highly successful in any area.**

The third step in C.H.A.OS is for You. Change. Now! the actions you need to take, the consistency of those actions, until they become Habits. That makes progress automatic!

- For each of the Fab Five, write the actions that you need to take to accomplish your goals
- Determine how often you need to take these actions to achieve your goals
- Begin to take the necessary actions in these key areas, continuing to reinforce these new ideals of action with your visualization and affirmations.

	Thoughts	What do you need to think?
	Words	What do you need to say?
	Actions	*What do you need to do?*
	Habits	*What needs to be automatic?*
	Character	What will you think of you?
	Reputation	What will others think of you?
	Destiny	Will that get you there?

What Do You Need To Accomplish *Financially?*

I need to focus on giving my best service in my current job and develop new skills to use in this position and future opportunities

I need to review my household finances and begin to look for opportunities to increase my revenue and lower expenses.

I need to begin to review financial statements of a select group of companies and determine which ones would be best to invest in.

Read books on business start-ups and look for a viable business to begin using my gifts, talents, and natural interests.

Research the cars I want to purchase and order a brochure to hang on my "dream wall".

Research and invest in software to model an investment portfolio of 100k before diving into the market on my own.

Exercise #9 - Action/Habits Make Success Automatic!

| Step 3 | C.H.A.O.S - Changing Habits Affecting OutcomeS |

HOW?
ACTION/HABITS!

Thoughts	What do you need to think?
Words	What do you need to say?
Actions	*What do you need to do?*
Habits	*What needs to be automatic?*
Character	What will you think of you?
Reputation	What will others think of you?
Destiny	Will that get you there?

What Do You Need To Accomplish *Financially*?

What Do You Need To Accomplish *Spiritually*?

What Do You Need To Accomplish *Mentally*?

What Do You Need To Accomplish *Physically*?

What Do You Need To Accomplish *Socially*?

Exercise #10 - Sample

Self - Image: A Better WHO Is HOW!

Self-Image is the true key to success. You must be able to see what others may not be able to see...*yet.* You must be able to percieve yourself *beyond* the immediacy of your current environment and situation.

The best reflection you can see in the mirror is an image that represents a life heading in the direction of a chosen purpose...even if you aren't there yet! The distance of the journey from **Thought to Destiny** becomes *shorter* when your **inner image is aligned with your desired outcome.**

The fourth step in C.H.A.O.S is to re-evaluate your **Character, Reputation, and Destiny** from the earlier results...*the change you have made already should amaze you!*

- Journal your response to the following questions, using your newly acquired (and yes, still developing!) thoughts, words, actions and habits.
  - What will you think about yourself as you make these changes in your life?
  - What will others begin to think of you as these efforts begin to show confirmation of change?
- If you consistently apply these new thoughts, words, actions, and habits, do you see yourself achieving your goals and dreams?

Thoughts	What do you need to think?
Words	*What do you need to say?*
Actions	*What do you need to do?*
Habits	*What needs to be automatic?*
Character	***What will you think of you?***
Reputation	***What will others think of you?***
Destiny	***Will that get you there?***

How Do You Need To See Yourself *Financially*?

As I am able to consistently apply the CHAOS method, I feel that I would have a better direction with my financial goals in life. It would make me more accountable. I would be more aware of what I am doing that is not consistent with my stated desires. It will take some time, but I can see how my image of myself will change slowly as I become more accustomed to thinking, speaking, and acting in accordance with the things I want. Others may see the change more quickly as I put these methods into practice. I am committed to showing up for work on time, taking on new assignments, and seeking new career opportunities as the cornerstone to a new financial future. I am committed to pursuing all avenues until I reach my ultimate destiny, which I now see as possible as I begin my transformation!!!

Exercise #10 – Self – Image: A Better WHO Is HOW!

Step 4	C.H.A.O.S - Changing Habits Affecting OutcomeS

HOW? SELF-IMAGE!

Thoughts	What do you need to think?
Words	What do you need to say?
Actions	What do you need to do?
Habits	What needs to be automatic?
Character	*What will you think of you?*
Reputation	*What will others think of you?*
Destiny	*Will that get you there?*

How Do You Need To See Yourself *Financially*?

How Do You Need To See Yourself *Spiritually*?

You. *Change.* Now!

How Do You Need To See Yourself *Mentally*?

How Do You Need To See Yourself *Physically*?

How Do You Need To See Yourself *Socially*?

JOURNAL, NOTES AND KEY LEARNINGS

_____

_____

_____

_____

_____

_____

_____

_____

_____

_____

_____

_____

_____

_____

_____

_____

_____

_____

_____

_____

_____

_____

_____

_____

_____

_____

_____

_____

_____

_____

_____

_____

_____

_____

_____

_____

_____

_____

_____

_____

_____

_____

_____

_____

Day 4 - Eliminate Fear

Fears are nothing more than a state of mind.
Napoleon Hill

To this point, we have focused on the mental challenges that people face in determining what they want out of life and the person they must become to achieve it. Now comes the true test – Action. Before we run out to conquer the world, there is one thing we need to address...**fear.** *Fear can actually serve a purpose, if we understand what it is, where it comes from, and how to overcome it.* Most people believe their visions are "just outside of their reach"...that their "dream is bigger than their ability". As was mentioned at the end of an earlier session, your only real requirement is to "Only be strong and of a good courage". Face it, fear is part of life – *no one is fearless.* Many people who *appear* fearless are able to manage fear with quick thoughts, decisions, and actions. **The difference between a coward and a brave man is that the brave man is not paralyzed by fear.** Fear insures that we think of all the possibilities an action can bring, but it should never stop us from taking action.

Many fears come by trying to leap into success too quickly. Diving in without all the facts makes us fall short and makes us look foolhearty. We try getting rich quick through schemes and investing in vehicles we don't understand. The result is perceived failure, when indeed, the idea or concept would have worked if you had been more aware of the pitfalls. This leads to bad experiences, which makes you fearful of another attempt.

Action is best taken in a series of progressive steps. The way may be paved with fear, but since moving forward is based on assessing all the given facts about a situation, fear can serve to make us wiser than if we acted "bravely" but foolishly.

Components of Fear

To tackle fear, you have to know what it consists of. If you search deep down, your fears are made up of 3 components. Understanding the root causes of fear will give you the insight to conquer it. Most fears are "built" from present circumstances, past experiences, and self-image.

1. **Present Circumstances** - People will look for every excuse for why they can't achieve success and live the life of their dreams. They may have every advantage necessary to move forward but will focus only on areas of deficiency. This form of "self-sabotage" creates the illusion that fate is against them. They are looking to place blame for their condition on outside influences and they never have to face the fact that they are responsible for their outcomes. The most common of these *present circumstance* excuses are:

   - Lack of resources – money, people, technology etc.
   - Physical issues – age, race, sex, etc
   - Lack of knowledge –education, experience
   - Lack of talent – gifts, background, previous success
   - Lack of desire – fear destroys ambition and creates inaction

   In your present circumstance are all the things you need to meet every challenge. In short, you are fully equipped for success! Your fears present the first opportunity to discover what it is you need in order to have victory.

2. **Past Experiences** - Past experiences provides you with the most convenient and compelling excuse for why you will not even *try* to succeed. History is indeed the best teacher of what we did wrong, **but it is also a reminder of what we did right.** For Thomas Edison,

1,000's of failures with the light bulb were *just enough!* Most people try something 3-5 times before getting it right. ***Persistence is the key!*** Have a conversation with someone who is "gun shy" about giving something another go, and they will likely describe something that can be tied to the past and two simple statements...*They have tried and failed or watched others fail.* <u>Understand that your history is not your destiny!</u> It is time to try again with a new frame of reference and a resolve to succeed!

3. <u>**Self Image**</u> - Of the three components of fear, self-image can be the most difficult to correct. These are fears and doubts created "between the ears". Some people will meditate on every possible reason they are not worthy to succeed and most of them have nothing to do with facts. Even with the advantages of resources, education and ideas, ***the insecure person will fail.*** However, once corrected, a powerful self-image will make up for issues in the first two components of fear. There are countless testimonies of people who have overcome true obstacles because they had a commanding self-image. They would not be refused due to lack of resources, physical challenges, or previous failures. *What is key to building a strong self-image?* Controlling thoughts, words, and actions are the key to destroying old images and replacing them with correct ones.

Once fear has been broken down into these three components it is more easily managed. Fear is a defense mechanism against acting foolishly, but ultimately, it is just False Evidence Appearing Real. The key is to bring negative thoughts of fear into captivity where you can keep an eye on them. **<u>Fears left to run wild will devour you and your dream!</u>**

Think about your major fears for each of the Fab Five. Look at your present, past and your inner self to see what really keeps you from taking action.

Once you discover the answers, you will be in a better position to handle fear. Our exercises are designed to help you learn more about yourself and the fears that keep you from living the life you described in great detail over the last couple of days. If you are still anxious, don't worry (no pun intended!), we have just begun to fight fear!

Remember, "only be strong and of a good courage". Addressing fears sends a message to the Triune Mind that you are *looking* for an answer and that you will act when that answer arrives. The super-conscious mind knows the answers and is waiting for you to *demand* that it be revealed. Stepping out in faith is the key that unlocks the vault of universal answers.

Bridges and Barriers

The Components of Fear that you uncovered are a fact of life. *However, they aren't the highest truth!* Gravity is a fact, but the law of lift supersedes it. For birds and bees, gravity is a fact, but flying is the truth for them. **For every barrier that is a fact in your life, there is a bridge that supersedes it.** Bridges may not be readily apparent, but they are there if you seek them out. Bridges are found by asking questions.

Building bridges in your *present circumstances* involves asking better questions than you are currently asking. What do I have today that can help me accomplish my goals? Is there an advantage to my physical appearance? Is the information I need available and where? What have I done in the past that would support this goal? Why is this "what" (desire) a must in my life? *The goal must be sufficiently strong in your mind that you will find answers and act on them once presented!*

Building bridges from your *past experiences* involves asking better questions. What lessons can I learn from my past? What role models can I see that have succeeded with challenges similar to mine? What small or large successes did I have in the past, even if I failed at the major objective? Ultimately, the past failures, or perceived failures must be removed. Forget those things behind you, and reach for the prize!

Our exercises will allow you to identify the barriers that are currently in front of you and the bridges that you need to build to "cross over". Allow your barriers to serve you with answers you need to eliminate fear. *Remember - for every barrier in your life, there is a bridge that can take you over to the Promised Land!* **Look for that bridge in every situation.**

What Must You Learn?

Once you have identified a Bridge, there is still information that you will need *before* you can act. It is the unknown, once a bridge is discovered, that keeps people from crossing. To provide a roadmap and insure that all is in place, we need to ask a few more questions and learn a few more things. Just like a reporter, who is investigating a story for the first time, we need to ask the basic questions:

Who? ~ What? ~ When? ~ Where? ~ How?

These types of questions get to the heart of what you must learn to insure that the activity you undertake will get you to your destiny! What do you need to learn before engaging in the activity? <u>After these learnings, what actions do you need to take?</u> This list of actions is traditionally referred to as a "Things To Do List". For some, "Things to Do" has a ring of drudgery to it — a common reason why so few people complete them! A better name would be a **"Things to Accomplish List"** since we actually want *To Accomplish* something when we engage in activity.

Lowest Common Denominator

No matter the size of the tasks, if it leads to the desired outcome, it is important! As you look at a "mountain of tasks", it is sometimes better to break it down into a series of smaller actions or the Lowest Common Denominator (LCD). The LCD is about breaking tasks down into their smallest component possible. Let's say that you want to make your first million in 6 years. For many, they just hit their M.S.P (Mental Sticking Point - *remember?*) just with the number $1,000,000. Let's break it down to it's LCD? The simple math:

$1,000,000 / 6 years = $167,000 a year - *still a BIG number (for some of you!)*

Let's continue breaking it down... Imagine you have a widget that you can create and sell on the internet (24/7 and 365 1/4) as a result of your natural gifts and passion. Let's assume the profit for each widget is $10 :

$167,000 / $10 profit = 16,700 units a year *(getting closer!)*

16,700 units / 365 days a year =

Average 45 units a day

Now you are no longer focused on a million dollars in 6 years, but selling an *average* of 45 units a day! Yes, some of you are still wrestling with how to sell 45 units a day, but even that can be broken down into its LCD (give it a try!)...*and at least now you are focused on 45 instead of $1,000,000!* Here is what is powerful about this type of eating the elephant "one bite at a time":

- Simple to the mind due to "smallest is easiest" approach.

- Allows action to be taken with no fear or limited fear since no <u>one</u> <u>action</u> is *too* big.

- Gives steady progress with small manageable steps.

- Continued "bite size" action demonstrates to the Triune Mind that you are serious about your future and builds your courage muscles to take grander action in the future.

All of these powerful concepts will help you Eliminate Fear and nothing will be impossible!

Exercise #11A - Sample

Fear - Eliminate the Distraction That Keeps You From Action!

Fear is to achievement, what gravity is to flight. An airplane, a bird, a bumblebee all need the force of gravity to aid them in flight. Though it is an *opposing force,* it provides the balance needed to successfully lift off the planet.

Fear has the same role in achievement. It provides the balance to make sure we do not act foolishly or without the proper facts. *The problem is that most people allow fear to paralyze them into inaction.* Moving past fear is the key to superior effort which will guarantee success!

Each fear we face can usually be de-constructed into 3 smaller components. These 3 Components of Fear - **Present Circumstances, Past Experiences, or Self-Image** offer a deeper insight into what holds us down and provides necessary leverage to overcome it!

- For each of the Fab Five area, identify 3 Major Fears that pose the greatest danger to pursuing your goals,
- For each of the Major Fears break them down into 3 Components of Fear. Take your time and analyze the true root causes of your fears.

Fear Elimination – Step 1
Identify What Creates Fear (Inaction) In Your Life?

Three Major Fears – Financial Goals

1. *Investing*	2. *Advancing career*	3. *Starting a business*
Three Components of Fear		
Fear of losing money	*Fear of inadequacy*	*Fear of no customers*
Fear of being "taken"	*Fear of change*	*Fear of economic conditions*
Fear of the market	*Fear of failure*	*Fear of competition*

Exercise 11B - Sample
Fear -Eliminate the Distraction That Keeps You From Action!

Now that you have identified the areas of fear, you need to begin to discover and uncover **Barriers and Bridges**. Yes, there are true Barriers that exist but for every Barrier there is a Bridge to crosss.

- Study each of your Components of Fear - **Write down the first Barrier that keeps you from action.**
- Immediately, write a **Bridge that can take you past the Barrier**. *Do not go forward until you have established a Bridge.*
- Continue writing Barriers and Bridges until you have covered each of your Components of Fear, or until you have exhausted every fear that exists in your life?

Fear Elimination – Step 2
Identify Bridges To Cross Every Barrier!

Financial Goals

Barriers	Bridges
Don't understand stocks	There are more resources available now than in any time in history to learn the market
What about recent crash and economic crisis	The best stocks have tripled since low point and many people have gotten wealthy despite conditions
I don't want to lose money	There are tools available to match investment style to risk profile
I don't trust stock brokers	Internet provides solid analysis and I can "trust but verify" the advice being given. I can also begin to "self invest" once I have the necessary knowledge

Exercise 11C - Sample

Fear - Eliminate the Distraction That Keeps You From Action!

With initial identification of Bridges, there is still additional evaluation to be conducted before you can act with confidence. Most fear is rooted in the "unknown", and most fears disappear with the enlightenment of knowledge. There are things you must learn and things you must do to propel you toward success!

Now that we have defined the "blueprint" of the Bridges needed in the previous exercise, we now need to gather the necessary raw materials (required knowledge in most cases) and begin to construct the Bridge for crossing over from Fear to Action. It is on the other side that all of our goals and dreams will be achieved.

For each Bridge, write the things that you must learn or do before you engage in specific activity. No learning is too small or trivial!

Remember, this indepth review and analysis is designed to ignite faith, destroy procrastination and to get you to remove all fear that distracts you from fulfillment!

Fear Elimination – Step 3
Building Bridges!

Bridges

What must be learned **What must be done**

Financial Goals

What Must Be Learned	What Must Be Done
Learn to read the financial papers	Research best online investment service
Analyze market returns after crashes	Study how puts protect a stock
Build a game plan for 1st million	Study how calls create income
Strategies to maximize 401k	Review 1 self made millionaire a week
Shift 5% of income to savings until 5k	Model mock investments online
Attend local investing workshop	Review possibility of real estate

Exercise #11A-C
Fear - Eliminate the Distraction That Keeps You From Action!

Step 1	Step 2	Step 3

Step 1: Major Fear → Present Circumstance, Past Experience, Self-Image

Step 2: Fears → Barriers, Bridges

Step 3: Bridges → What must be learned, What must be done

Three Major Fears – Financial Goals

1	2	3

Three Components of Fear

1	2	3
1	2	3
1	2	3

Barriers	Bridges

What Must Be Learned	What Must Be Done

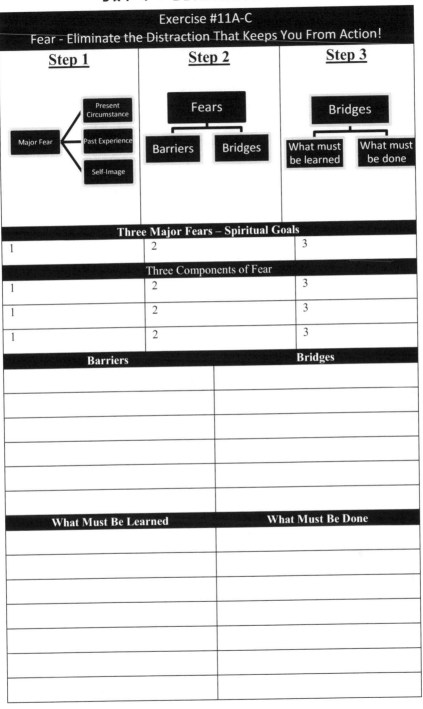

Exercise #11A-C
Fear - Eliminate the Distraction That Keeps You From Action!

Step 1	Step 2	Step 3

Three Major Fears – Spiritual Goals

1	2	3

Three Components of Fear

1	2	3
1	2	3
1	2	3

Barriers	Bridges

What Must Be Learned	What Must Be Done

Exercise #11A-C
Fear - Eliminate the Distraction That Keeps You From Action!

Step 1	Step 2	Step 3

Three Major Fears – Mental Goals		
1	2	3

Three Components of Fear		
1	2	3
1	2	3
1	2	3

Barriers	Bridges

What Must Be Learned	What Must Be Done

Exercise #11A-C
Fear - Eliminate the Distraction That Keeps You From Action!

Step 1	Step 2	Step 3

Step 1: Major Fear → Present Circumstance, Past Experience, Self-Image

Step 2: Fears → Barriers, Bridges

Step 3: Bridges → What must be learned, What must be done

Three Major Fears – Physical Goals		
1	2	3

Three Components of Fear		
1	2	3
1	2	3
1	2	3

Barriers	Bridges

What Must Be Learned	What Must Be Done

Exercise #11A-C
Fear - Eliminate the Distraction That Keeps You From Action!

Step 1	Step 2	Step 3

Three Major Fears – Social Goals		
1	2	3

Three Components of Fear		
1	2	3
1	2	3
1	2	3

Barriers	Bridges

What Must Be Learned	What Must Be Done

JOURNAL, NOTES AND KEY LEARNINGS

_____

_____

_____

_____

_____

_____

_____

_____

_____

_____

_____

_____

_____

_____

_____

_____

_____

_____

_____

_____

_____

_____

_____

_____

_____

_____

_____

_____

_____

_____

_____

_____

_____

_____

_____

_____

_____

_____

_____

_____

_____

_____

_____

_____

_____

Day Five - Focus On A Goal

*Focus on the journey, not the destination. Joy is found
not in finishing an activity but in doing it. Only one thing
has to change for us to know happiness in our lives:
where we focus our attention.*
Greg Anderson

Congratulations! You have proven yourself as one of the elite regarding success behavior. While this program is only 7 days, many people have already quit, but you are determined to see this through till the end. *Surprised?* <u>Even with the power of the concepts presented here, and the simple way it's delivered, most people stop before it's over.</u> **Why?** The answer is not because they don't want to succeed, they just lack what is today's topic – Focus. More commonly known as Discipline.

What is discipline? Traditionally, discipline has a negative connotation. Say the word discipline to a child and they will say "when daddy spanks me". Even when discipline is engaged to reach a favorable outcome, it still has a twinge of negativism. It speaks of arduous labor that we detest but that we must do with dogged focus to accomplish a desired goal. The traditionally thought of definition is wrong. Let's evolve our vocabulary and meaning of discipline. Let's see it as the willing servant that creates a focus on **what we want, what it takes to get there, and a commitment to see it through to the end.** New definition of discipline:

Doing what it takes, to get what you want…
as long as it takes, until you get what you want!

Thinking/Planning/Acting

In order to make focusing efficient, there is a three-part strategy that must be implemented. We can become what we desire by utilizing the triumvirate (think tricyle!) of **Thinking, Planning, and Acting.**

- **Thinking** – Gives you the vision of where you want to go. Thinking is the process of preparing your self-image with the tools it needs to understand your intentions, and building the mental confidence that **it will happen**. With this system, the "thinking" sessions are <u>Elevate Your Mind</u>, and <u>Activate the Triune Mind</u>. These sessions focus on creating the receptivity to enlarging your world and the things you believe you can create within it. It introduces you to using imagination to fuel your inner passion.

- **Planning** – Gives you the strategy to get there. Planning is the process where you begin to take the images presented to your Triune Mind and turn them into tangible strategies and tactics. With this system, the "planning" sessions are <u>Strategize</u> and <u>Eliminate Fear</u>.

- **Acting** – Starts, continues, and finishes the journey. Acting is the final stage in the ongoing process of the Evolution to Completion. **Acting is more than just doing daily tasks.** It involves the "act" of fear elimination, creation of a specific plan, and execution of that plan. With this system, the "acting" sessions are <u>Focus on a Goal</u>, <u>Master Money</u>, and <u>Achieve Balance</u>.

There is tremendous synergy between these three activities. Thinking delivers you to a plan, the plan gives you confidence to act, which stimulates more thinking, which stimulates planning…until you get what you want! In order to keep them in balance, there is a recommended ratio to maintain:

10% Thinking, 15% Planning, and 75% Acting

We all know people who do nothing but daydream about the future. Ask them where their plans are and they are "working on them". We all know people who act without planning. They are notorious for saying, "maybe next time I will get lucky and get it right". The ratio of 10% Thinking, 15% Planning, and 75% Acting is critical to insure that once you gain momentum, *you maintain it*. **Ultimately, the ability to remained focused on your goals will determine the magnitude of success you achieve**.

Exercise #12 - Sample
Focus on Goal

Step One	Step Two	Step Three
Write in your top three short term goals. Insert your signature as a sign of your commitment to being disciplined to accomplish all that is necessary to see your goals fulfilled!	Using the results from the Fear Elimination exercises, develop the series of actions you need to take to achieve these desires with appropriate level of priorty (1-4) with 1 being the most urgent.	Determine a specific date by which each action will be taken and completed. Hold yourself to these dates and avoid procrastination!

Planning to Succeed!

What I Want Financially	*I am committed to doing what it takes to get what I want, as long as it takes, until I get what I want!*
1. 100k salary	
2. Start business	*Signed Brandon L. Clay*
3. Invest 10k	

Priority	Action	Target Date
1 2 3 4	Post for new internal position in sales	1/1/2011
1 2 3 4	Update resume and gather necessary industry information	1/1/2001
1 2 3 4	Wake up daily and watch Squawk Box on CNBC before leaving for work	1/1/2001
1 2 3 4	Save 5% of salary, add to current savings ($1,000) and accumulate $2,500	4/1/2011
1 2 3 4	Set up a self managed account with XYZ brokerage with $2,500 initial investment	4/15/2011
1 2 3 4	Put 100k in mock online account and follow trades for next 90 days to track results	4/20/2011
1 2 3 4	Call Uncle Bill and invite him to lunch and pick his brain on starting a business	6/1/2011
1 2 3 4	Develop the initial ideas for my business and create a 3 year business outline	4/1/2011
1 2 3 4	Read 3 success books and begin doing research on successful entrepreneurs on the internet	2/1/2011

Exercise #12 - Focus On A Goal

What I Want Financially	*I am committed to doing what it takes to get what I want, as long as it takes, until I get what I want!*
1.	
2.	*Signed* _____
3.	

Priority	Action	Target Date
1 2 3 4		
1 2 3 4		
1 2 3 4		
1 2 3 4		
1 2 3 4		
1 2 3 4		
1 2 3 4		
1 2 3 4		
1 2 3 4		
1 2 3 4		
1 2 3 4		
1 2 3 4		
1 2 3 4		
1 2 3 4		
1 2 3 4		

Exercise #12 - Focus On A Goal

What I Want Spiritually	*I am committed to doing what it takes to get what I want, as long as it takes, until I get what I want!*
1.	
2.	*Signed* _____
3.	

Priority	Action	Target Date
1 2 3 4		
1 2 3 4		
1 2 3 4		
1 2 3 4		
1 2 3 4		
1 2 3 4		
1 2 3 4		
1 2 3 4		
1 2 3 4		
1 2 3 4		
1 2 3 4		
1 2 3 4		
1 2 3 4		
1 2 3 4		
1 2 3 4		

Exercise #12 - Focus On A Goal

What I Want Mentally	*I am committed to doing what it takes to get what I want, as long as it takes, until I get what I want!*
1.	
2.	*Signed* _____
3.	

Priority	Action	Target Date
1 2 3 4		
1 2 3 4		
1 2 3 4		
1 2 3 4		
1 2 3 4		
1 2 3 4		
1 2 3 4		
1 2 3 4		
1 2 3 4		
1 2 3 4		
1 2 3 4		
1 2 3 4		
1 2 3 4		
1 2 3 4		
1 2 3 4		

Exercise #12 - Focus On A Goal

What I Want Physically	*I am committed to doing what it takes to get what I want, as long as it takes, until I get what I want!*
1.	
2.	*Signed* _____
3.	

Priority	Action	Target Date
1 2 3 4		
1 2 3 4		
1 2 3 4		
1 2 3 4		
1 2 3 4		
1 2 3 4		
1 2 3 4		
1 2 3 4		
1 2 3 4		
1 2 3 4		
1 2 3 4		
1 2 3 4		
1 2 3 4		
1 2 3 4		
1 2 3 4		

Exercise #12 - Focus On A Goal		
What I Want Socially	*I am committed to doing what it takes to get what I want, as long as it takes, until I get what I want!*	
1.		
2.	*Signed* _____	
3.		
Priority	**Action**	**Target Date**
1 2 3 4		
1 2 3 4		
1 2 3 4		
1 2 3 4		
1 2 3 4		
1 2 3 4		
1 2 3 4		
1 2 3 4		
1 2 3 4		
1 2 3 4		
1 2 3 4		
1 2 3 4		
1 2 3 4		
1 2 3 4		
1 2 3 4		

DAY 5 - FOCUS ON A GOAL

JOURNAL, NOTES AND KEY LEARNINGS

_____

_____

_____

_____

_____

_____

_____

_____

_____

_____

_____

_____

_____

_____

_____

_____

_____

_____

_____

_____

DAY 5 - FOCUS ON A GOAL

You. *Change.* Now!

Day Six - Master Money

Wealth flows from energy and ideas.
William Feather

Finally, a discussion on money! What I have discovered is that people who focus on money *first*, have a hard time acquiring it! Taking care of your mental power, developing goals (*in balance* with the Fab Five), analyzing tools to conquer fear and developing a strong self-image had to be first priorities *before* a discussion on money would be received properly.

The Bible says to "seek first the kingdom and all these other things will be added to you" - Matthew 6:33. That kingdom resides on the *inside of you*...it is a mental and spiritual awareness of who you are and what you <u>desire and deserve</u>. It makes you aware of your right to be successful in every area of your life and that you are fully capable of manifesting money. This section on money mastery has powerful techniques and strategies for the accumulation of wealth. **Not designed as a course on money management but a course on becoming a money magnet!**

Who typically creates and manages their money best? Major corporations who are ***accountable*** to build earnings for stock growth, to a board of directors, and to shareholders. These corporations hire dozens of people to do nothing but monitor the revenue and expenses of their organization. The Chief Financial Officer (CFO) is vital to the financial health and well being of billion dollar concerns. *Why don't you run your household corporation the same way?* Commit to running your household finances like a Fortune 500 company!

Given the current challenges in our world economy, financial vigilence is no longer a luxury but a necessity. Make no mistake, income and wealth opportunities are plentiful but can no longer be found in the "usual places". For the typcial person, the home equity lines of credit, easy job transitions/raises/promotions, or "dart throwing" stock picks are a thing of the past to create "certain wealth". In these challenging times, only the companies (that means you - the corporation!) that have taken a hard look at their balance sheets, products and services, and made tough decisions have survived. The first priority of any company is to increase the top line - revenue. The only way to increase earnings is to do one of two things, *but preferably both*:

Increase Revenue *and/or* Lower Expenses

Let's begin building the correlation between how a corporation reviews its finances and how *you* should run your household enterprise:

- **Increase revenue** - Of course, this is your income from all sources and is the primary means of operating your household. To raise your standard of living and to begin to create wealth (money mastery) you need to increase your revenue. How do major corporations raise their top line? Let's review:

  o **Price increases** - Certainly, if you could earn more in your profession that would be a good thing...*right?* ***How do you feel when your favorite product has a price increase?*** Not so good...*unless* of course, it is a "new and improved" version! No one likes to pay more for the same product...they want improvement for the premium in price. You have to do the same thing...become more valuable (new and improved!) to create the mandate of higher pay!

  o **New products** - Companies do research on a continual basis to determine if brand loyalty opens the door for insertion of additional products into their current line. For example, a dozen years ago, I used to buy razors, shaving cream, and skin care items from multiple companies. Now, I buy all of the products in an integrated skin care "system" - <u>from one company</u>! Can you add a second job, create addtional income from a part-time hobby, or begin a business to augment your current 9 to 5 product line?

- o **<u>Merger and Acquisitions</u>** - In order to be more competitive and leverage "economies of scale", companies will join forces. This consolidation of infrastructures and products can even create a monopoly where all consumers have to get the widget *exclusively* from this union. This creates revenue favorability and a stronger corporation. Are you putting off a union...*yes, a hint for marriage*, waiting for things to "get better"? While prudence and financial preparedness is necessary *before* nuptials, waiting for economic conditions to be perfect is counter-productive. Are you in a marriage where you operate individually as separate "small" companies...*my money, your money*? **That system is a recipe for disaster** (bankruptcy - business failure to keep the metaphor going). Bringing two together will always provide synergy to increase the opportunities available *versus* single concerns.

- o **<u>Investments for passive income</u>** - Most people are unaware that most large corporations make as much revenue from investing in real estate, stocks (yes, of other companies!), new technologies (Research & Development), and other investments to increase their revenue and ability to withstand economic winds of change. This makes them more impregnable and less suspect to the ups and downs of their primary business...*plus they receive major tax favorability for doing it!!!* Can you invest in real estate, stocks, 401k, and small businesses as a way to create passive income? Passive income works when you don't...it is *"make it while I sleep"* money...**a good thing!** It just so happens that the I.R.S will give you some of the same breaks it gives big corporations for creating this stream of revenue.

- **Lower Expenses** - Once your top line is established and maximized, we need to view the way we *spend* that revenue. Let's review how corporations manage their expenses:

  o **Budget creation and management** - Several months *before* the beginning of each year, a corporation will create a budget that will become the "final word" on how they will operate in the coming year. If there are any significant negative variances (spending more than planned) then immediate action is taken - **no excuses**. You will even see some companies "freeze" 4th quarter hiring, raises, travel, etc. to get the budget back in line before the end of year. They have to report their annual budgets to shareholders and make quarterly accounting for all revenue and expenses. While creating a budget is not alway sexy, having money (profit!) left over at the end of the year, is!

  o **More efficient production** - There are top management courses that do nothing but focus on how efficiently a corporation develops, builds, and distributes its products. To save 5% on the cost of delivery of a good or service doesn't sound like much until you think in terms of millions or billions of dollars. Where can you save money on your monthly necessities and luxuries? Are the luxuries *appropriate* based on your balance sheet? It will be necessary to review **every** expenditure and ensure that you have maximized the value of that item while minimizing its cost.

o **Debt restructure and borrowing** - There are times when the "cost of money" is favorable and corporations will leverage their good credit and revenue position to restructure their debt or borrow for expansion of their business. In former economic "good times", borrowing to re-finance to lower rates (credit cards, cars, and houses), was a no brainer. In this period of low rates but tight money, wisdom and prudence is necessary so as not to create more future economic turmoil. Now, debt creation should only be used if it creates a dramatically lower expense proposition **(with a corresponding change in debt habits!)** or to build/expand a business that will ultimately generate more revenue.

Large corporations do other things that you should do for your household corporation. They hire professionals when the need arises - lawyers, advisors, experts, etc. We all need advice in some area of our lives and finances can be complicated...don't be afraid to "hire" your weaknesses! Corporations also market their business to get the word out about how great their product is to drive consumer behavior. Madison Avenue spends billions of dollars building images and status for their clients. *You are a product, whether you are working for someone or if you are a business owner.* Hone your image, work to convey the characteristics you want to "sell" to the world. **More people will "buy" who you are, the value you provide, and in return will help you increase your revenue!**

Begin to review your finances frequently, at least 2 times a month. Identify trends that are hurting your bottom line and take actions as if your company could go belly-up if you didn't. *In fact, it could!* Once you have a firm grip on your current balance sheet, it is time to focus on increasing the top line of revenue. The key to real wealth generation is the ability to "create" money. There are two concepts we need to engage for Money Mastery:

Triangle of Wealth & The Power of 2

Two simple concepts that by themselves, can yield amazing results, but when used *together*, they can create millions in anyone's lifetime! Before we examine these concepts, let's review what most people have...a Triangle of Death (yes, graphic!).

Triangle of Death

The Triangle of Death is the opposite of the Triangle of Wealth. Unfortunately, this is the most common form of "living" that is killing people day by day. It represents all revenue coming from our primary jobs. We pay all expenses and enjoyment (if any!) from this *limited* pool of funds. It doesn't matter how high the revenue is, **we tend to live right at the top of it**. If there is anything left, we save. Nearly impossible to accumulate any real wealth this way, and creates a form of "slavery" to our profession. We are typically one disaster away from financial challenges or ruin because all of our revenue is derived from <u>one source</u> and we spend ALL of that revenue on our lifestyle. *There is a better way!*

The Triangle of Wealth

To make your household corporation impregnable, it is vital for you to have multiple streams of revenue (income). The **Triangle of Wealth** is made up of three components - Profession, Passion, and Passive revenue. Profession revenue is money earned from your current vocation. Passion revenue is money earned from your "calling" and that which you love and yearn to do and become. Finally, Passive revenue is money earned "while you sleep", typically residual income from previous efforts (book royalties for example) and investments such as stocks and real estate.

As you begin to create your Triangle of Wealth, you will create an *immediate* increase in revenue! That additional revenue, driven by the addition of Passion and Passive activities, will be directed into your wealth building vehicles. These vehicles will *get your money to make more money* (yes, increased Passive revenue!). They will become the mechanism that will drive the next concept, **The Power of 2**, and will multiply your household corporate earnings (*your wealth!*) like never before! As you transition from *profession only* earnings, your life will be more enjoyable and you will have achieved the real measure of success – <u>**Living life totally on your own agenda!**</u>

<u>Creating The Triangle of Wealth</u>

In our exercises after this section we will evaluate where your Triangle of Wealth percentages are today. Then, regardless of where it is today, we are now going to establish future targets. As you do the exercises, don't allow the dramatic rise in figures to intimidate you. On average, going from ***Today*** to the ***Phase Three Target*** means tripling your income! You have inside of you, right now, the gifts and abilities to increase your revenue. **You. *Change.* Now!** is about recognizing and uncovering those gifts. It is designed to help you develop a plan, to map out the direction you need to go to create "The Possible Future"...let's continue:

Phase One	Phase Two	Phase Three	Phase Four
• 85% - Profession	• 70% - Profession	• 40% - Profession	• 80% - Passion
• 10% - Passion	• 20% - Passion	• 40% - Passion	• 20% - Passive
• 5% - Passive	• 10% - Passive	• 20% - Passive	

Phase Four is the "ultimate phase" for the **Triangle of Wealth** and gives you the opportunity to break the ties of your profession and make a great living from your own gifts and talents. Granted, this is not for everyone, but it is a dream for millions of people who consider this the ultimate freedom! Be diligent with the exercises and work on your personal calculations for the various phases of your Triangle of Wealth! Doing these calculations will show you what is possible and you will break through your M.S.P (Mental Sticking Point)...that alone makes it vital to your financial success!

The Power of 2

Once you have revenue that is not earmarked for expenses, you need to make that revenue grow through investments (passive income). The **Power of 2** is a simple, time-tested concept that determines how *fast* your hard earned revenue increases! The concept - multiply **one** dollar times **two** and the outcome is, of course, **two dollars**. Multiply $1,000 times two and the result is, you guessed it...$2,000. Any number times two *doubles* that number. The number 2 is the lowest whole number that you can multiply by and see growth.

Power of 2 Basics

- Provides steady growth

- Easy on the mind

- First cycle and last cycles are the slowest (requires you to get started and finish strong)

- Middle cycles are the fastest (due to inertia and momentum)

The Magic Penny - The Power of Compounding

Ever heard of the concept of the Magic Penny? It holds the key to explosive wealth. If you had a penny that doubled (Power of 2) everyday for 30 days it would become $5,368,709.12. *How is this possible?* It revolves around the concept of compounding, which Albert Einstein declared was the 9th wonder of the world. For the Power of 2 concept, each time the penny doubles is referred to as a "cycle". The first cycle takes one penny and it increases to two pennies. The 15th cycle creates $164. The 25th cycle creates $167,772 and finally, the 30th cycle leaves you with over 5 million dollars. That is truly magic!!! Let's apply that "magic of compounding" to a current savings of $1,000 and see what happens using the Power of 2.

- ➢ Begin with $1,000
- ➢ Cycle 1 - $2,000
- ➢ Cycle 2 - $4,000
- ➢ Cycle 3 - $8,000
- ➢ Cycle 4 - $16,000
- ➢ Cycle 5 - $32,000
- ➢ Cycle 6 - $64,000
- ➢ Cycle 7 - $128,000
- ➢ Cycle 8 - $256,000
- ➢ Cycle 9 - $512,000
- ➢ At the end of the 10th cycle you have $1,024,000!!!

How Long Does Each Cycle Last?

Once people understand the Power of 2 concept and the amazing results that are possible, their first question is *"How Long Does Each Cycle Last?"*. Fair question. Remember the old math problem, "if one train leaves the station at 3:00pm and another at 5:00pm…?" Part of the answer to that question involves the equation:

$$Distance = Speed \times Time$$

- o **Distance** is the size of your desire – how far and how rich you want to be.
- o **Speed** is the effective effort you are willing to give.
- o **Time** is the *variable* of how long it will take to get there.

to solve for time (*how long will it take*) the equation becomes:

$$Time = Distance/Speed \text{ or}$$

$$How\ Long = How\ Rich\ /\ Your\ Effort$$

The Need For Speed!

Using the last version of the equation, the factor that is most influential on how long each cycle will last is *your effort*. While the Magic Penny is fascinating, the notion that you could double your money every day is not realistic. In the real world, compounding *leverages* time to do its work. Albert Einstein is also credited with creating a simple formula for determining how fast your money will double in an interest bearing environment. It is called the Rule of 72 and is as follows:

72 ÷ the interest rate received on an investment = number of years for your money to double

Let's review a more traditional view of how that rule impacts the time of each cycle:

Annual Interest Earned on Investment	2%	4%	6%	12%	24%
How long *per cycle* "Rule of 72"	36 years	18 years	12 years	6 years	3 years
Value of $1,000 after 36 years	$2,000	$4,000	$8,000	$64,000	$4,096,000

As you can see, the interest rate (speed) you receive on your "working money" determines how long each cycle lasts (time) and how much your money grows (distance). The contrast between 2% and 24% is startling, and everyone would immediately be drawn to the $4 million outcome of 24%. Certainly, there are people achieving great returns but in the "real world" of risk/reward, each individual will be governed by their financial ability and financial fears. You can put your money in the stock market, you can expand your business, you can invest in real estate or some combination of them all to grow your money. One thing is for certain, putting it "in the ground" is not going to make it grow! Here are a few factors that will determine how fast you will progress through the Power of 2 cycles:

- **Knowledge** – *Yes, the more you know the faster your money will grow.* George Soros and Warren Buffet have earned billions for themselves and others with their outerworldy knowledge of financial instruments, companies, and trends. As described in Strategize (Day 3), you can choose these men or others to model as your financial heros, or you can trust them to do the investing for you (Berkshire Hathaway is still traded!). If you entrust your money to professionals, you will still need knowledge to make sure you are not blindly trusting *anyone* with your money - think of Bernie Madoff or the fresh out of college money manager who is using your account to "learn the trade"! Basic knowledge of what you are investing in is required to keep your advisors honest.

- **Resources** – The more resources you have access to will accelerate your wealth building endeavors. In this new age of information and innovation, you do not have to be born with the "silver spoon", or on the "right side of the tracks". There are enough raw materials available to anyone that is focused, to build wealth. What is at your disposal right now? Do you need to obtain specialized knowledge? The libraries and internet are vast information storehouses. Do you have a computer? You can research the various ways to grow your revenue...from real estate, multi-level marketing, to writing a novel. *The resource of information can not be your excuse!!!* Financial resources will be necessary as the "seed" of your future money harvest, but that seed will come as the result of some form of knowledge. When resources *seem* scarce, use inspiration, innovation, and intention to create that "wealth seed" and plant it in good ground.

- **Ideas** – One idea can create millions (yes, even billions) *"overnight"*. As was mentioned in the first day of this program, **each** of us has a ready made audience for the gifts and talents we are blessed with. **The key to uncovering and discovering that value is through ideas.** The great thing about ideas, is that one idea gives birth to another, and another...until the idea grows from a simple "eureka" moment to a full fledged movement! When ideas come, think on them, give thanks for them and, when required, *act boldly on them* - they will be the fuel for your wealth engine.

- **Courage** – As it relates to the compounding effect of money, the **earlier** you start a program, the better. You have likely heard the story of two brothers...one began saving $100 a month from age 20 to age 30...that is 10 years of saving. The other brother procrastinated due to fear and other factors, but "saw the light" at age 30. He saved the same $100 from age 30 to age 65 - a total of 35 years. Assuming both earned the same interest rate, who do you think had more money at age 65? *Actually, at age 65, they have essentially the same amount of money.* However, the first brother who started earlier but only "sowed seed" for 10 years, got there with a lot less effort. When it comes to the Power of 2 and the time component of each cycle, he who hesitates usually arrives late!

- **Discipline** – Knowledge, resources, and ideas can only bear the fruit of wealth *if* you do them, consistently. Are you contributing every pay period to your 401k, dollar cost averaging into the stock market, and reaching out to 5 contacts a day to grow your business? Doing the daily activities necessary, *until* they become a habit is the hallmark of discipline. These strong money habits will serve to provide momentum for your money locomotive! The more disciplined you become, the faster the cycles.

Exercise #13 - Sample
Cash Flow Analysis

Summary

	Budgeted	Actual	Variance	Notes
Total Income	A. $6,850	A. $6,850	A. $0	Target $500 more income
Total Expenses	B. $6,388	B. $5,952	B. +$436	Target $300 cuts next 90 days
Profit / Loss	A-B +$462	A-B +$898	A-B +$436	Increased savings to $900!

Revenue Analysis

	Budgeted	Actual	Variance	Notes
Gross Salary	6,250	6,250	0	
Commission / Bonuses				
Investment Income				
Other	600	600	0	Part time position on weekends
Total Income	A. $6,850	A $6,850	A 0	

Expense Analysis

Withholdings	Budgeted	Actual	Variance	Notes
Federal Income Tax	1,300	1250	50	
State Income Tax	425	419	6	
FICA Withholding	375	355	20	
401K Deduction	50	50		
Healthcare Deductions	68	68		
Other Deductions				
Total Withholdings	2,218	2,142	+76	
Housing	**Budgeted**	**Actual**	**Variance**	**Notes**
Primary Mortgage	950	950	0	
Secondary Mortgage				
Property Taxes				

Home Insurance				
Furnishing/ Decorating	200	150	50	Strict budget until complete!
Other Housing Expenses	75	0	75	Cancel service...cut myself!
Total Housing	1,225	1,110	+115	

Automobile	Budgeted	Actual	Variance	Notes
Auto Loan #1	450	450	0	
Auto Loan #2				
Auto Insurance	125	100	25	Shopped for lower rates
Gasoline	125	125	0	
Repairs/ Maintenance	65	65	0	
Other Auto Expenses				
Total Automobile	765	740	+25	

Financed	Budgeted	Actual	Variance	Notes
Credit Card #1	55	55	0	Balance of $2100
Credit Card #2	75	75	0	Balance of $3000
Credit Card #3				
Credit Card #4				
Consumer Loans	105	105	0	Two more payments!
IRS Payments				
Other Payments				
Total Financed Expenses	235	235	0	

Utilities	Budgeted	Actual	Variance	Notes
Electricity	125	90	35	Went to budget billing
Natural Gas	45	25	20	Off season rates
Telephone Mobile Phone	75	45	30	Better call plan!
Internet/ Cable TV	50	50	0	
Garbage Collection	15	15	0	

Water/Sewer	30	30	0	
Other Utilities				
Total Utilities	340	255	+85	
Living	**Budgeted**	**Actual**	**Variance**	**Notes**
Food – Groceries	350	300	50	*Yes...Coupons!*
Food – Dining Out	125	50	75	*Lower budget*
Charitable Donations	150	150	0	
Childcare	400	400	0	*Open FSA with employer in 2011*
Clothing	250	250	0	
Entertainment	80	80	0	
Travel				
Education				
Fitness	100	100	0	
Gifts				
Insurances				
Parking	55	55	0	
Personal Care	95	95	0	
Pet Care				
Other				
Total Living	1,605	1,480	125	
Total Expenses	**Budgeted**	**Actual**	**Variance**	**Notes**
	B. $6,388	B. $5,952.00	B. +$436	

Exercise #13 - Cash Flow Analysis

Summary

	Budgeted	Actual	Variance	Notes
Total Income	A. $	A. $	A. $	
Total Expenses	B. $	B. $	B. $	
Profit / Loss	A-B $	A-B $	A-B $	

Revenue Analysis

	Budgeted	Actual	Variance	Notes
Gross Salary				
Commission / Bonuses				
Investment Income				
Other				
Total Income	A.	A	A	

Expense Analysis

Withholdings	Budgeted	Actual	Variance	Notes
Federal Income Tax				
State Income Tax				
FICA Withholding				
401K Deduction				
Healthcare Deductions				
Other Deductions				
Total Withholdings				
Housing	Budgeted	Actual	Variance	Notes
Primary Mortgage				
Secondary Mortgage				
Property Taxes				
Home Insurance				
Furnishing/ Decorating				

Other Housing Expenses				
Total Housing				

Automobile	Budgeted	Actual	Variance	Notes
Auto Loan #1				
Auto Loan #2				
Auto Insurance				
Gasoline				
Repairs/ Maintenance				
Other Auto Expenses				
Total Automobile				

Financed	Budgeted	Actual	Variance	Notes
Credit Card #1				
Credit Card #2				
Credit Card #3				
Credit Card #4				
Consumer Loans				
IRS Payments				
Other Payments				
Total Financed Expenses				

Utilities	Budgeted	Actual	Variance	Notes
Electricity				
Natural Gas				
Telephone Mobile Phone				
Internet/ Cable TV				
Garbage Collection				
Water/ Sewer				
Other Utilities				

Total Utilities				
Living	**Budgeted**	**Actual**	**Variance**	**Notes**
Food – Groceries				
Food – Dining Out				
Charitable Donations				
Childcare				
Clothing				
Entertainment				
Travel				
Education				
Fitness				
Gifts				
Insurances				
Parking				
Personal Care				
Pet Care				
Other				
Total Living				
Total Expenses	**Budgeted**	**Actual**	**Variance**	**Notes**
	B.	B.	B.	

Exercise 14 - Sample
Triangle of Wealth - Today

Passive Income – Money that works, even when you don't!

List all annual passive income in column on the right. Add up the total and insert in the Summary below in Passive Income "**Amount**"

Type	Amount
Residual Income	$
Stocks/Bonds	$ 1,000
Real Estate	$
Business System	$
Retirement Income	$
401k Match	$ 2,500
Other	$
Total	$ 3,500

Passion Income – Do what you love, and the money will follow!

List all annual passion income in column on the right. Add up the total and insert in the Summary below in Passion Income "**Amount**"

Type	Amount
Business	$
Part-time	$
Hobby	$ 5,000
Other	$
Total	$ 5,000

Profession Income – Making the most of 9-5

List all annual Profession income in column on the right. Add up the total and insert in the Summary below in Profession Income "**Amount**"

Type	Amount
1st Profession	$ 45,000
2nd Profession	$ 30,000
Other	$
Total	$ 75,000

Triangle of Wealth Summary

Source	Amount	Passive	Passion	Profession
Passive Income	$ 3,500	Passive income Total Divided by Total Income X 100 = Passive Percentage	Passion Income Total Divided by Total Income X 100 = Passion Percentage	Profession Income Total Divided by Total Income X 100 = Profession Percentage
Passion Income	$ 5,000			
Profession Income	$ 75,000			
Total Income	$ 83,500	4 %	6 %	90 %

Exercise #14
Triangle of Wealth - Today
Passive Income – Money that works, even when you don't!

Type	Amount
Residual Income	$
Stocks/Bonds	$
Real Estate	$
Business System	$
Retirement Income	$
401k Match	$
Other	$
Total	$

Passion Income – Do what you love, and the money will follow!

Type	Amount
Business	$
Part-time	$
Hobby	$
Other	$
Total	$

Profession Income – Making the most of 9-5

Type	Amount
1st Profession	$
2nd Profession	$
Other	$
Total	$

Source	Amount	Passive	Passion	Profession
Passive Income	$	Passive Total Divided by	Passion Total Divided by	Profession Total Divided by
Passion Income	$	Total Income X 100 =	Total Income X 100 =	Total Income X 100 =
Profession Income	$	Passive Percentage	Passion Percentage	Profession Percentage
Total Income	$	%	%	%

Exercise #15 - Sample

Triangle of Wealth - Phase One

Profession	Passion	Passive
85%	**10%**	**5%**
Projected Professional Income	Total Target Income x .10 = Target Passion Income	Total Target Income x .05 = Target Passive Income
$80,000	$9,411	$4,705
Divided by .85 =		
Target Total Income		
$94,117		

Triangle of Wealth - Phase Two

Profession	Passion	Passive
70%	**20%**	**10%**
Projected Professional Income	Total Target Income x .20 = Target Passion Income	Total Target Income x .10 = Target Passive Income
$85,000	$24,285	$12,143
Divided by .70 =		
Target Total Income		
$121,428		

Triangle of Wealth - Phase Three

Profession	Passion	Passive
40%	**40%**	**20%**
Projected Professional Income	Total Target Income x .40 = Target Passion Income	Total Target Income x .20 = Target Passive Income
$90,000	$90,000	$45,000
Divided by .40 =		
Target Total Income		
$225,000		

Phase	Profession	Passion	Passive	Total Income
Today	$75,000	$5,000	$3,500	$83,500
Phase One	$80,000	$9,411	$4,705	$94,117
Phase Two	$85,000	$24,285	$12,143	$121,428
Phase Three	$90,000	$90,000	$45,000	$225,000

Exercise #15
Triangle of Wealth – Phase One

Profession	Passion	Passive
85%	**10%**	**5%**
Projected Professional Income	Total Target Income x .10 = Target Passion Income	Total Target Income x .05 = Target Passive Income
$	$	$
Divided by .85 = Target Total Income		
$		

Triangle of Wealth – Phase Two

Profession	Passion	Passive
70%	**20%**	**10%**
Projected Professional Income	Total Target Income x .20 = Target Passion Income	Total Target Income x .10 = Target Passive Income
$	$	$
Divided by .70 = Target Total Income		
$		

Triangle of Wealth – Phase Three

Profession	Passion	Passive
40%	**40%**	**20%**
Projected Professional Income	Total Target Income x .40 = Target Passion Income	Total Target Income x .20 = Target Passive Income
$	$	$
Divided by .40 = Target Total Income		
$		

Phase	Profession	Passion	Passive	Total Income
Today	$	$	$	$
Phase One	$	$	$	$
Phase Two	$	$	$	$
Phase Three	$	$	$	$

Exercise #16 - Sample

The Magic Penny

The pupose of this daily exercise is to keep you focused on increase. While this exercise may seem "juvenile/simplistic", once your mind becomes focused on increase and "doubling" your current resources, it will provide you with inspiration and guidance on how to achieve it!

On Day 1 start with a "Magic Penny". Recite the **Magic Penny Affirmation** each day and begin reviewing current and future "Source of Funds" to get to the next day's amounts. When you get "stuck" on a day don't despair, continue to affirm that your Magic Penny is preparing to double and soon enough...it will!!! Project the next achievement date and stay focused.

Magic Penny Affirmation

I gave thanks for all of my financial blessings and the amount of (current assets). I give thanks for the knowledge, abilities, and wisdom necessary to double this money with my appropriate effort by (target date). I receive the increase of (insert next amount needed) now!

Day #	Amount	Target Date	Source of Funds
Day 1	$0.01	1/1/2011	Son found penny in street!
Day 2	$0.02	1/2/2011	Found in car seat
Day 3	$0.04	1/3/2011	Found in car seat!
Day 4	$0.08		Found in car seat!
Day 5	$0.16	No source of money should go untapped!	Found in car seat
Day 6	$0.32		Money from couch
Day 7	$0.64		Change from fast food
Day 8	$1.28		Money found in washer
Day 9	$2.56	1/9/2011	Loose in kitchen drawer
Day 10	$5.12	1/10/2011	Change in valet in closet
Day 11	$10.24	1/11/2011	Skipped a coffee/lunch out
Day 12	$20.48	1/12/2011	Rented movie not theatre
Day 13	$40.96	1/13/2011	Rebate software purchase
Day 14	$81.92	1/14/2011	Money in Saving
Day 15	$163.84	1/15/2011	Money in Savings
Day 16	$327.68	1/16/2011	Money in Savings
Day 17	$655.36	1/17/2011	Money in savings
Day 18	$1,310.72	1/18/2011	Money in savings
Day 19	$2,621.44	1/19/2011	Money in Mutual Funds
Day 20	$5,242.88	1/20/2011	401k vested balance
Day 21	$10,485.76	1/21/2011	Cash value of insurance
Day 22	$20,971.52	1/1/2012	Raise, lowered expenses
Day 23	$41,943.04	6/1/2012	Started business
Day 24	$83,886.08	1/1/2013	Business income, raises
Day 25	$167,772.16	6/1/2013	$200k total income
Day 26	$335,544.32	1/1/2014	Full time in business!!!
Day 27	$671,088.64	6/1/2014	Expanded to 5 new markets
Day 28	$1,342,177.28	1/1/2015	Launch national platform
Day 29	$2,684,354.56	1/1/2016	Expanded products!!!

Here, Day 21 represents a "sticking point". Strategy and persistence is necessary

Represents a five year net worth goal!

Exercise #16 - The Magic Penny!			
Day #	Amount	Target Date	Source of Funds
Day 1	$0.01		
Day 2	$0.02		
Day 3	$0.04		
Day 4	$0.08		
Day 5	$0.16		
Day 6	$0.32		
Day 7	$0.64		
Day 8	$1.28		
Day 9	$2.56		
Day 10	$5.12		
Day 11	$10.24		
Day 12	$20.48		
Day 13	$40.96		
Day 14	$81.92		
Day 15	$163.84		
Day 16	$327.68		
Day 17	$655.36		
Day 18	$1,310.72		
Day 19	$2,621.44		
Day 20	$5,242.88		

Day 21	$10,485.76		
Day 22	$20,971.52		
Day 23	$41,943.04		
Day 24	$83,886.08		
Day 25	$167,772.16		
Day 26	$335,544.32		
Day 27	$671,088.64		
Day 28	$1,342,177.28		
Day 29	$2,684,354.56		
Day 30	$5,368,709.12		
Day 31	$10,737,418.24		
Day 32	$21,474,836.48		
Day 33	$42,949,672.96		
Day 34	$85,899,345.92		
Day 35	$171,798,691.84		
Day 36	$343,597,383.68		
Day 37	$687,194,767.36		
Day 38	$1,374,389,534.72		

Magic Penny Affirmation

I gave thanks for all of my financial blessings and the amount of (current assets). I give thanks for the knowledge, abilities, and wisdom necessary to double this money with my appropriate effort by (target date). I receive the increase of (insert next amount needed) now!

Day Seven - Achieve Balance

*Be aware of wonder. Live a balanced life - learn some
and think some and draw and paint and sing and dance
and play and work every day some.*
Robert Fulghum

The most important concept of all is Achieving Balance. While this is the shortest session, it is the most vital as it will determine the *intensity* of true happiness in life. Most people miss this concept as they live out their lives in a series of "priorities". Chasing money for a while, then focusing on losing weight, and when it "fits", being attentive to their spouse/family, etc. The key to a life well-lived is pursuing <u>all areas</u> of the Fab Five, *with balance*, and progressing a little in each area every day.

Make no mistake, the Fab Five are interrelated, and pursuing one area to the detriment of others will create an imbalance. **Each area affects the others.** A majority of people put the most pressure on themselves financially. What usually happens in this single-minded pursuit, is they experience loss in the other four areas. Mentally, they become obsessed to the detriment of clear thinking. Socially, they lose sight of loved ones and friends resulting in high divorce rates and no one to share their victories with. Phycially, they gain weight, and develop poor health habits. Spiritually, they commit no time to getting to know God, themselves, or the world around them.

I can hear many people saying, *"I don't have time to do all of the things required to live a balanced life"*. **That is not true.** I understand that working takes the first 40+ hours a week of your life. Eating and sleeping take another 65 hours. When you factor in the things outside of work you *have to do*, there appears to be no time for achieving balance. I would push back and ask, "How long does it take to reflect on the day ahead and the one just ending? *Couldn't you "spare" 10 minutes (lying in bed) in* *the morning and evening to meditate on the day that is/was/will be?* No time to play with the kids? What if the first 15 minutes when you got home from work was devoted to playing a simple game of checkers, Scrabble, or listening to their music (hey, you might find out you like it!)? The point, is that there is always time to do a **little of everything**...and everything is important! First rule of life...people will <u>always</u> find time to do those things they want to do (or deem important enough). Sometimes, it is simply a matter of "connecting the dots".

<u>Connect the D.O.T.s</u>

To address the genuine concern of a lack of time, or what is ultimately, a lack of time management, I would like to introduce one last concept - DOTs, where:

- **"D" is for Desire** - As we learned from the **Activate the Triune Mind** session (Day 2), the driving force of desire is "What" we want combined with "Why" we want it. If constructed properly, the two create a white heat of desire that compels us to act in a way that is consistent with the attainment of our vision. We create an imbalance when the "Why" is not of sufficient emotional importance/value to drive us to act in a consistent (habitual) manner. For example, if you want a better relationship with your spouse, you might *say* it is important, but the emotional urgency is not enough to make you do all the right things consistently - spending quality time in conversation, sharing intimacy, planning and dreaming together, etc. In essence, as you chase other higher priorities, you "take for granted" that you can always come back to them when everything else is in order. What if your spouse said that they were leaving you, or you suspected they were "cheating"...how might that impact the "Why" of your desire? **It would become urgent and you would want to repair the damage.** We should not operate our lives in "crisis management" mode all the time, instead, each area of our lives should have sufficient value to mandate its inclusion in our daily routines. If there is a "What" goal (Exercise 4A) that is not getting proper attention in your life, go back to the "Why" (Exercise 4B) and develop and create higher meaning!

- **"O" for Opportunity** - When you have established that something is important to your quality of life, the opportunity to engage in it <u>always</u> emerges. If the business plan is critical to your future success and freedom from your current job, then you will wake up early, or stay up late to create the opportunity to pursue it. Same thing for your physical workouts...you will create the opportunity. It may not be the optimum time of day or week, but until you have *complete control* of your time (which no one ever really does!), you will have to take advantage of windows of opportunity. Think of your life like TIVO ® , the technology that allows you to record your favorite shows and watch them when you have opportunity...at your convenience. What a novel idea! Just like the concept of TIVO ® , your life can't always be reflective of a television schedule, where a murder can happen at 7:06pm and be neatly concluded at 7:57pm! For example, I love golf and it is important to me, but my normal week is filled with other things, and I want to be with family on the weekends. The courses I play began a program - "9 by 9" - where I can play 9 holes (as opposed to a full 18)and be finished before 9am. Yes, I have to get up at 6am and brave the dark and sometimes cold, but since golf is of "emotional importance", I made the opportunity life change. For the things that are vital, you will have to "get them in where they fit it", but look for the opportunites - they will emerge!

- **"T" is for Time -** We are all working with the same 24 hours and 7 days a week. Of course, some people are maximizing that time and accomplishing amazing things. You may not be able to devote <u>all</u> the time you would like to everything you need/want/have to accomplish but can you find better ways to accomplish more in the time you have available? *Can you delegate some of the things that require your time?* As you increase financially, can you pay for someone to cook, clean, detail your car, or run errands? The people that maximize their time, don't spend it in the mundane (chores), they utilize their time to create more life experiences. Can you begin doing the new, more intense physical workouts that take 30 minutes, rather than the standard treadmill for an hour routine? Can you do it at home and save 30 minutes getting to and from the gym? The important thing is to understand that time is a precious commodity and not to waste any of it!!!

Enjoy the Ride!

Achieving balance is essential to living the "charmed life", and requires you to value each day, each moment, and **relish the journey more than the destination**. I occasionally reflect on something that Mr. Spock said in the classic Star Trek episode "Amok Time" (1967). He had just killed Captain Kirk in an epic Vulcan "death match" for the hand of T'Pring, his betrothed. The apparent death of his captain immediately dissipated his desire for T'Pring, who had conspired to marry another man. Mr. Spock, in his trademark logical fashion, turned to the man she fancied and simply said (and I paraphrase), "There is more pleasure in the wanting, than the having". His statement reflects a paradoxical, counter-intuitive philosophy, but one that afflicts many people. They don't take the time to "smell the roses" of daily life but strive only to put the roses in a vase - not appreciating the growth process. We need to consult the emotional side of ourselves as well as the Mr. Spock "logical" side and allow them to blend into a full view of life.

That is the ultimate purpose of the **You. *Change.* Now!** system - to assist you in living your life in such a way that achievement is not anticlimactic, but that you have so many great things to look forward to, that your life is a supreme adventure. A journey that will be filled with joy and pain, challenges and triumphs, but ultimately, can be viewed as a life well lived. Review the things you have done the last 6 days, and continue to review and refine them as the pages of your life turn in your own perfect Evolution to Completion.

I stand in agreement that every wonderful thing you desire will manifest perfectly, and that serendipitously, one day our paths will cross and we can have a good old-fashioned testimony session. Thank you for allowing me to be part of your change!

DAY 7 - ACHIEVE BALANCE

About Brandon L. Clay

Brandon L. Clay is an author/story-teller, international speaker, and sales leader. For the past 28 years, he has delivered his distinctive brand of instruction and inspiration to over 30,000 sales professionals and 1,000's of others outside the sales arena. His strength is that he understands that there is no standardized template or "cookie cutter" approach to creating high sales achievers. His power of connection allows him to recognize and leverage each person's unique talents and help them unleash their greatest potential.

Inspired by his father-in-law, LeRoy Shuffler, and combined with his experience of the 1,000's of people touched and transformed by his unique combination of life and sales mastery, he penned **Sales Crumbs from the Master's Table.** Brandon's entertaining, empowering, and enlightening approach to coaching sales excellence is brought to life through this simple story. It quickly become regarded as a *must read* for anyone in sales and inspired the follow-up volumes in the Trilogy - **A Trail of Sales Crumbs** and **Feasting On Sales Crumbs**. This trilogy is now touching everyone from CEO's, VP's, managers, seasoned veterans, to "newbies" in their first week and helping him fulfill his mission of Helping Millions Achieve Success...One At A Time.

He lives in McDonough, Georgia with his high school sweetheart, Natalie, and their 3 children, Chaz, Christian, and Faith.

Learn more about Brandon, his available programs and additional resources at

www.brandonlclay.com

Additional Titles Available from Brandon L Clay;

<u>Sales Crumbs Trilogy</u> – *the definitive guide to sales success and life mastery!*

Volume I - Sales Crumbs from the Master's Table

Volume II - A Trail of Sales Crumbs

Volume III - Feasting On Sales Crumbs

Your Authentic Sales Voice - *Discovering and unleashing your most natural gift for greater sales success!*

S=ME² - *Revolutionary Success Formula!*

The 80% Sales Solution - *Training program based on the popular Sales Crumbs Trilogy*

Made in the USA
Charleston, SC
06 March 2014